# Astrological Keywords

A Reference Manual

Pam Fleuret

Copyright 2016 by Pam Fleuret
All rights reserved.

No part of this book may be reproduced or transcribed in any form or by any means, electronic or mechanical, including photocopying or recording or by any information storage and retrieval system without written permission from the author and publisher, except in the case of brief quotations embodied in critical reviews and articles. Requests and inquiries may be mailed to: American Federation of Astrologers, Inc., 6535 S. Rural Road, Tempe, AZ 85283.

ISBN-10: 0-86690-665-7
ISBN-13: 978-0-86690-665-4

Cover Design: Jack Cipolla

Published by:
American Federation of Astrologers, Inc.
6535 S. Rural Road
Tempe, AZ 85283

www.astrologers.com

This book is dedicated to my husband, Dave,
and children Kevin, Keith and Tiffany for their help and encouragement.

Also my Sister, Mom, and Grandma for their support and participation in my endeavors.

# Contents

| | |
|---|---|
| Introduction | vii |
| A to Z Keywords | 1 |
| Keywords for Signs | 101 |
| Keywords for Houses | 127 |
| Keywords for Planets | 157 |
| Keywords for Aspects | 187 |
| Part of Fortune | 189 |
| Asteroids and Nodes | 191 |
| References | 193 |

# Introduction

"The keyword system is the most efficient means by which the student of astrology can analyze the implications of a horoscope with the depth of understanding and breadth of appreciation."— Manly P. Hall, *Astrological Keywords*.

This reference book was designed as a tool to be used in conjunction with instructional books.

Why did I assemble this book about keywords alone? The book started out as a personal tool and grew and grew. Who would have thought that there would be a need for a keyword for worms, and yet my niece went into the business of teaching people about crop fertilization using worms. The use of this book with natal, transit, horary, and election charts will help provide speedy and sound reports.

Beginners will find as they look through the houses, signs, and planets, that they will discover the essence of each. This will make it much easier to read a chart. For the teacher it will be a useful tool.

**Helpful Tips**
In the astrological keyword section the numbers 1 through 12 indicate the first house through the twelfth house in an astrological chart.

The querent is the person who is asking the question in a horary or election chart.

The symbols (glyphs) are:

**Signs**
- ♈ Aries
- ♉ Taurus
- ♊ Gemini
- ♋ Cancer
- ♌ Leo
- ♍ Virgo
- ♎ Libra
- ♏ Scorpio
- ♐ Sagittarius
- ♑ Capricorn
- ♒ Aquarius
- ♓ Pisces

**Planets**
- ☉ Sun
- ☽ Moon
- ☿ Mercury
- ♀ Venus
- ♂ Mars
- ♃ Jupiter
- ♄ Saturn
- ♅ Uranus
- ♆ Neptune
- ♇ Pluto
- ☊ North Node
- ☋ South Node

**Aspects**
- ☌ Conjunction
- ☍ Opposition
- □ Square
- △ Trine
- ✶ Sextile
- ⋎ Semi-Sextile
- ⚻ Quincunx
- ∠ Semi-square
- ⚼ Sesquisquare
- ∥ Parallel
- ⚹ Contra-Parallel

**Chiron and Lilith**
- ⚷ Chiron
- ⚸ Lilith

**Asteroids**
- ⚳ Ceres
- ⚴ Pallas
- ⚵ Juno
- ⚶ Vesta

You may wonder why are there so many indications for each keyword. Take the word "research" for example.

Research: 8, 12, Pluto, Neptune, Gemini

Gemini might wish to research for fun or just to gain knowledge. The eighth house could indicate research of an accounting nature to keep debts in order. The twelfth house and Pluto might indicate research for a hospital. Then there is Neptune, which could indicate what you are doing now, researching astrology, or maybe there is a secret involved. You need to determine into which area the question would fall.

Getting a feeling for the signs, houses, and planets will give you the reasons for the keywords in your charts.

A student might look at each placement as a fill-in-the-blank kind of model.

Ruler (Keyword) Sign (Keyword) House (Keyword) Sign (Keyword)

Ruler (Keyword) Aspect (Keyword) Planet (Keyword) Sign (Keyword)

## Sample Natal Charts Using the Keyword System:

The following example charts show how you could use the Keyword System to fill in the blanks making it easier to read a chart. In these examples, I am only using the major aspects for simplicity sake. The examples use the system as follows:

- Planet (Keyword)
- Sign (Keyword)
- House (Keyword)
- Aspect (Keyword)
- Planet (Keyword)
- Sign (Keyword)

## Mother Teresa

*Sun*

- Sun (Achievement, Generosity, Honors, Integrity) in
- Virgo (Analysis, Fears Disease and Poverty, Study) in the
- Eighth House (Compulsions, Famine, Obsessions, Shrewdness)
- Trine (Ease)
- Saturn (Discipline, Hard Work, Organizational Ability)
- Sextile (Affability, Attraction)
- Pluto (Hospitals, Intensity, Nuns, Regeneration)
- Trine (Ease)
- Ascendant (Ambitions, Appearance, How Others See the Individual)
- Interpretation of Mother Teresa's Sun: There are many people who do important charity work, but few gain the recognition that Mother Teresa did. For a woman working in the slums of Calcutta, she received an amazing amount of recognition, including The 1979 Nobel Peace Prize, and in 2003 she was beatified as "Blessed Teresa of Calcutta."

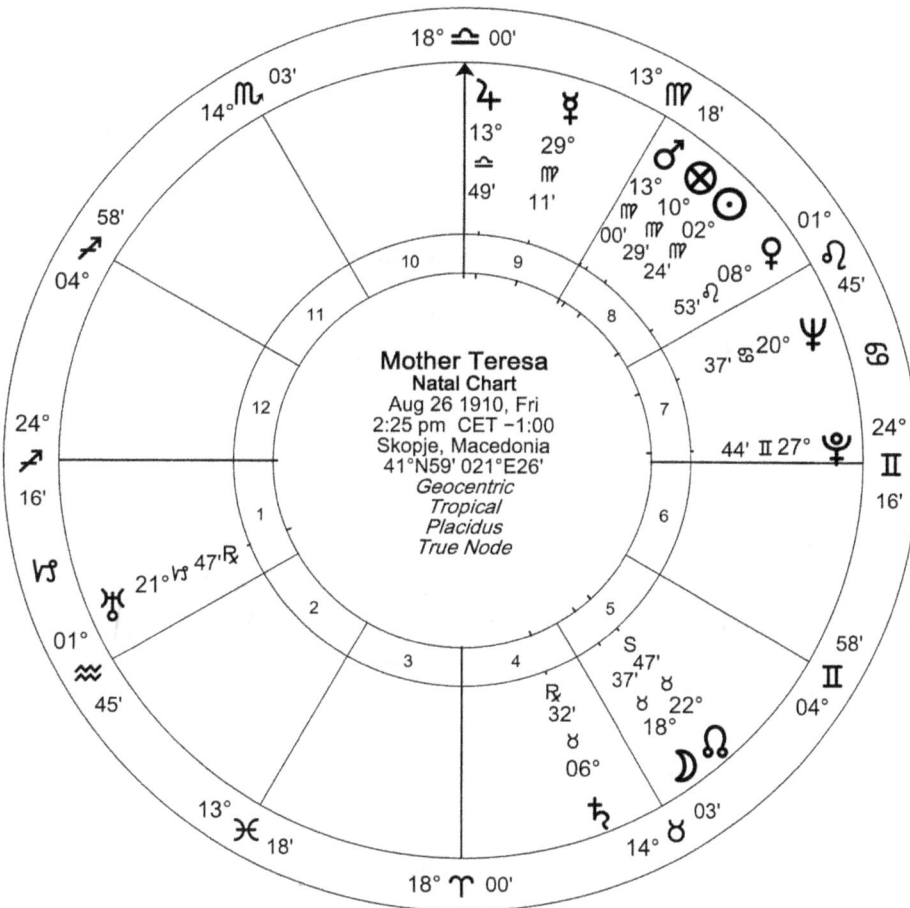

Was it luck? The Keyword System indicates that she was born to be honored for her great work. Using this system let us see why she became the great Mother Teresa. It starts with her Sun sign, which focuses not just on good works but achievement and honors. Placed in Virgo, you can see that she chose to work in the area indicated by that sign: people with diseases and those who live in poverty. In the eighth house you find the qualities that helped Mother Teresa to be more than a person who helped those in need. It indicates a shrewdness, a person with a great ability to attract others to her in work with the sick and the poor. The trine with Saturn, according to the Keyword System, shines a light on discipline and organizational ability. The sextile with Pluto emphasizes the ability to attract other people to a cause, with a clear connection to religion and a passion for helping with those who experience great suffering. The trine to the Ascendant indicates she modeled a certain behavior of calm, carrying a belief that even one person can make a difference. As others saw her dedication, she was offered support for her causes.

The keyword analysis of her Sun sign focuses on her ability to attract attention to her causes and to organize others to support these causes; in turn, she received recognition for her work.

### *Moon*

- Moon (Dealings with the Public, Notoriety, Women) in
- Taurus (Dependable, Idealistic, Loyal) in the
- Fifth House (Educational Pursuits, Passions)
- Trine (Ease)
- Mars (Initiative, Strength, Passions)
- Trine (Ease)
- Uranus (Autonomy, Humanitarian, Progressive Thinking)

- Sextile (Affability, Attraction)
- Neptune (Ascetic, Charities, Compassion)
- Interpretation of Mother Teresa's Moon: The Moon's ability allowed her to gain loyalty from others and to draw from her own inner strength. She was dependable and loyal to her charities. She attracted others to her cause and always kept the big picture in her sights.

### *Mercury*

- Mercury (Communication, Cleverness, Education, Linguistic Ability, People Who Give Service) in
- Virgo (Analysis, Fears Disease and Poverty, Study) in the
- Ninth House (Scholars, Religious Affairs, Church, Teaching)
- Square (Accomplishment, Tension)
- Pluto (Hospitals, Intensity, Nuns, Regeneration)
- Square (Accomplishment, Tension)
- Ascendant (Ambitions, Appearance, How Others See the Individual)
- Interpretation of Mother Teresa's Mercury: Mother Teresa was clever and had a strong linguistic ability; she spoke five languages. The Keyword System highlights her path to working with people who had the greatest suffering. She found support through her church and her belief system. Philosophy and religion occupied her thoughts.

### *Venus*

- Venus (Affairs of the Heart, Comfort, Diplomacy) in
- Leo (Children, Creative, Optimistic, Plagues) in the
- Eighth House (Compulsions, Famine, Obsessions, Shrewdness)
- Sextile (Affability, Attraction)
- Jupiter (Academic Success, Altruism, Faith, Charities, Churches, Success)
- Square (Accomplishment, Tension)
- Saturn (Discipline, Hard Work, Organizational Ability)
- Interpretation of Mother Teresa's Venus: This placement indicates that Mother Teresa would naturally have a special interest in helping children, as well as people of all ages with communicable and life threatening diseases. Mother Teresa was noted for her work with people who had AIDS, HIV, leprosy, and tuberculosis. Venus also reiterates Mother Teresa's organizational ability and her modeling self-discipline.

### *Mars*

- *Mars* (Initiative, Strength, Passions) in
- Virgo (Analysis, Fears Disease and Poverty, Study) in the
- Eighth House (Compulsions, Famine, Obsessions, Shrewdness)
- Trine (Ease)
- Moon (Dealings with Public, Notoriety, Women)
- Trine (Ease)
- Saturn (Discipline, Hard Work, Organizational Ability)
- Interpretation of Mother Teresa's Mars: Mother Teresa had a passion to help those who were suffering great illnesses and those living in great poverty. We see the repetition of ease (trine), when her life didn't seem easy. The trine represents her ability to attract others to help her, easing her own work through her ability to raise compas-

sion in others and to organize many workforces. The keywords indicate that Mother Teresa would be bright and she was very bright. She spoke five languages, became a teacher at the Loreto convent and taught for nearly 20 years, eventually becoming headmistress of the convent. Many would consider her an accomplished woman, but with achievement and honors so dominant in her chart, these accomplishments were not enough for her. A passion burned inside of her, a passion to not only lessen the suffering in this world but to raise compassion and good works in others. Her chart indicates that her discipline, organizational ability, and recognition that she had to fight for those who could not fight for themselves made it possible for her to make a great difference in this world—not only in her lifetime but for ever more. Mother Teresa was not afraid to be recognized as the most famous charity worker in the world, a model for us all.

### Jupiter

- Jupiter (Academic Success, Altruism, Faith, Charities, Churches, Success) in
- Libra (Cooperative, Peace Loving, Persuasive) in the
- Ninth House (Scholars, Religious Affairs, Church, Teaching)
- Sextile (Affability, Attraction)
- Venus (Affairs of the Heart, Comfort, Diplomacy)
- Square (Accomplishment, Tension)
- Neptune (Ascetic, Charities, Compassion)
- Conjunction (Concentration, New Venture)
- Midheaven (Achievement, Fame, Authority and Authority Figures)

• Interpretation for Mother Teresa's Jupiter: Mother Teresa used qualities of persuasiveness, diplomacy, and high moral character to convince others to help with her causes. She was not afraid to ruffle a few feathers with those she wanted to convince, and her strong convictions, moral authority and public image most often won the support of those who were reluctant.

### Saturn

- Saturn (Discipline, Hard Work, Organizational Ability) in
- Taurus (Dependable, Idealistic, Loyal) in the
- Fourth House (Community, Home, Common People)
- Trine (Ease)
- Sun (Achievement, Generosity, Honors, Integrity)
- Square (Accomplishment, Tension)
- Venus (Affairs of the Heart, Comfort, Diplomacy)
- Trine (Ease)
- Mars (Initiative, Strength, Passions)

• Interpretation of Mother Teresa's Saturn: Mother Teresa was a hard worker and a representative of the common people. Tension was sometimes an issue when she couldn't get the cooperation and support her work required.

### Uranus

- Uranus (Autonomy, Humanitarians, Progressive Thinking) in
- Capricorn (Practical, Responsible, Stubborn) in the
- First House (How Others See the Individual, Temperament, Self-Confidence)
- Trine (Ease, Achievement, Generosity, Honors, Integrity)

- Moon (Dealings with Public, Notoriety, Women)
- Opposition (Destructive)
- Neptune (Ascetic, Charities, Compassion)
- Square (Accomplishment, Tension)
- Midheaven (Achievement, Fame, Authority and Authority Figures)

• Interpretation for Mother Teresa's Uranus: She, in her enthusiasm, conflicted with those in authority over her humanitarian goals, but keywords illustrate she used her stubbornness and passion to help her accomplish her goals. The first year she began her missionary work (1948) she had extreme difficulty getting what she needed. She had to beg for food and supplies, but she never gave up.

### Neptune

- Neptune (Ascetic, Charities, Compassion) in
- Cancer (Charity Organizers, Maternal, Sympathetic) in the
- Seventh House (Common People, Associates, Cooperation)
- Sextile (Affability, Attraction)
- Moon (Dealings with Public, Notoriety, Women)
- Square (Accomplishment, Tension)
- Jupiter (Academic Success, Altruism, Faith, Charities, Churches, Success)
- Opposition (Destructive)
- Uranus (Autonomy, Humanitarian, Progressive Thinking)
- Square (Accomplishment, Tension)
- Midheaven (Achievement, Fame, Authority and Authority Figures)

• Interpretation for Mother Teresa's Neptune: Her organizational ability, progressive thinking, faith, and a focus on accomplishment allowed her to balance a wide range of activities and manage 4,000 sisters to run her orphanages, AIDS hospices, and charity centers, and to care for refugees, the blind, disabled, aged, alcoholic, poor, homeless, and victims of floods and epidemics and famine, not only in Calcutta but all over the world.

### Pluto

- *Pluto* (Hospitals, Intensity, Nuns, Regeneration) in
- *Gemini* (Adaptable, Clever, Inventive) in the
- *Seventh House* (Common People, Associates, Cooperation)
- *Sextile* (Affability, Attraction)
- *Sun* (Achievement, Generosity, Honors, Integrity)
- Square (Accomplishment, Tension)
- Mercury (Communication, Cleverness, Education, Linguistic Ability, People Who Serve)
- Opposition (Destructive)
- Ascendant (Ambitions, Appearance, How Others See the Individual)

• Interpretation of Mother Teresa's Pluto: Pluto shows how Mother Teresa used her inventiveness to accomplish so much in one lifetime, often conflicting with the powers-that-be. She didn't care what others thought, she had her eyes on what she wanted for her charities and that was what mattered.

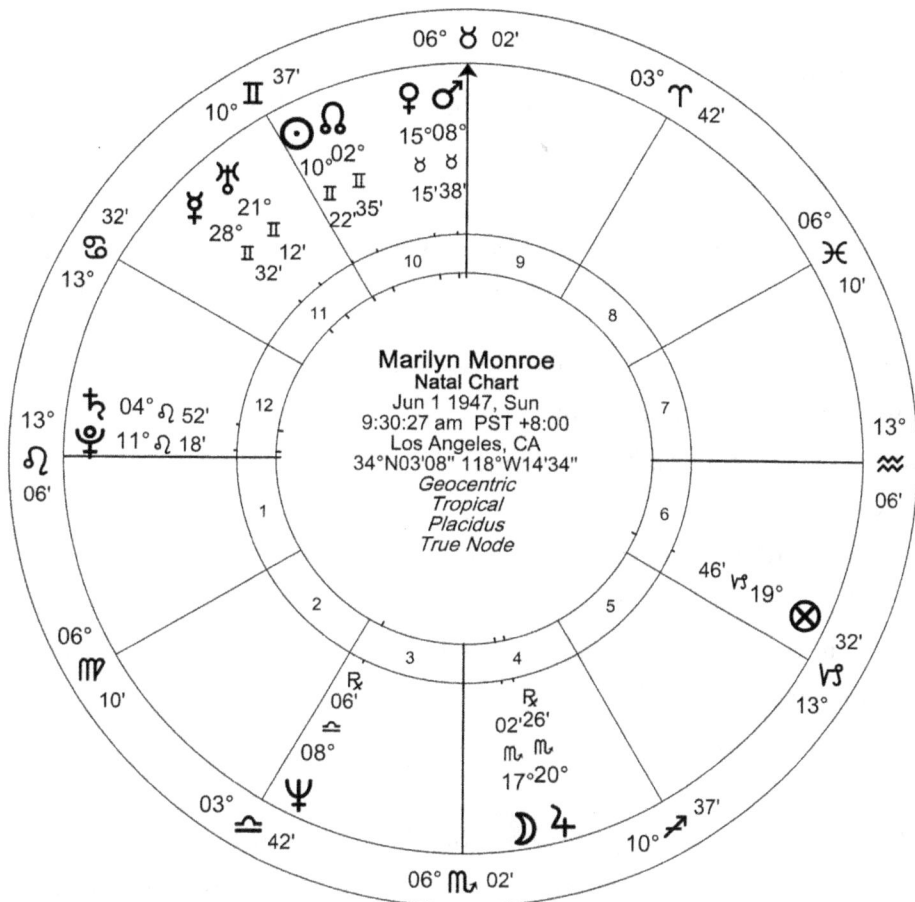

Mother Teresa was ambitious and she had a goal: to help the sick and the poor. To do this she had to be shrewd, determined, organized, and ambitious. She didn't care what anyone thought of her. She was out to help as many people as she could and if this involved great recognition, that was a plus. What would have happened if she did not have this strong theme of accomplishment and honor in her chart highlighted by the Keyword System?

## Marilyn Monroe

### Sun

- Sun (Achievement, Acting, Creative Talent) in
- Gemini (Adaptable, Childlike, Intellectual, Talkative) in the
- Tenth House (Achievement, Ambitious, Business Affairs, Infamy)
- Sextile (Affability, Attraction)
- Saturn (Achievement, Ambition, Bondage, Hard work)
- Trine (Ease)
- Neptune (Acting, Glamor, Orphanages)
- Sextile (Affability, Attraction)
- Pluto (Movies, Sexuality)
- Sextile (Affability, Attraction)
- Ascendant (Ambitions, Appearance, How Others See the Individual)

xiii

- Interpretation for Marilyn Monroe's Sun: Marilyn's Sun sign correlates closely with her biography. Although she seemed naïve, innocent and gullible, Marilyn was anything but these. Abandoned by her mother at a young age, abused and molested over several years in the foster care system, she learned how to survive. Her gifts of attractiveness combined with her high intellect and acting ability, both in the real world and in the movies, helped her to create an image that was both sexual and entertaining. A distinctive image established her as an icon and not just an actress. But these tools could not save her. Her early experience of betrayal and abuse led to a lifetime of difficult relationships. Even as a successful actress, feelings of bondage, or being trapped, remained part of her life. Many interviews with her expressed her frustration of not being able to escape the image she created and the movies perpetuated. Marilyn's natural talent, intellect, and ambition made her dissatisfied with just being a star.

## *Moon*

- Moon (Emotional Needs, Family, Women) in
- Scorpio (Passionate-Resourceful-Sex) in the
- Fourth House (Family, Emotional Needs, Home)
- Opposition (Destructive)
- Venus (Love, Female Relations, Love Affairs, Partner)
- Conjunction (Concentration, New Venture)
- Jupiter (Education, Good Fortune, Professional Ability)
- Square (Accomplishment, Tension)
- Pluto (Abuse, Betrayal, Sex)
- Square (Accomplishment, Tension)
- Ascendant (Ambitions, Appearance, How Others See the Individual)

• Interpretation for Marilyn Monroe's Moon: Keywords for Marilyn's Moon are similar to those of her Sun. However, the keywords for her Moon focus more on her need to feel loved and to be happy in a relationship. Her difficulty in finding love and happiness were probably connected to her early and tragic death at 36 years of age.

## *Mercury*

- Mercury (Cleverness, Communication, Education) in
- Gemini (Adaptable, Childlike, Dual) in the
- Eleventh House (Idea of Happiness, Income from Business or Career, Receiving Love)

• Interpretation for Marilyn Monroe's Mercury: Marilyn's chart again shows that she was clever and could communicate with those she wished to in a very effective way. She had a movie career and was also a model, indicating a dual career.

## *Venus*

- Venus (Love, Female Relations, Love Affairs, Partner) in
- Taurus (Dependable, Idealistic, Practical) in the
- Tenth House (Achievement, Ambitious, Business Affairs, Infamy)
- Opposition (Destructive)
- Moon (Emotional Needs, Family, Women)
- Conjunction (Concentration, New Venture)
- Mars (Assertiveness, Competition, Courage)
- Opposition (Destructive)

- Jupiter (Education, Good Fortune, Professional Ability)
- Square (Accomplishment, Tension)
- Pluto (Abuse, Betrayal, Sex)
- Square (Accomplishment, Tension)
- Ascendant (Ambitions, Appearance, How Others See the Individual)

• Interpretation of Marilyn Monroe's Venus: Her Venus shows good fortune and the ability to make money and keep money. It repeats the Sun sign's problems in keeping good relationships. It also emphasizes women and family, which must have been very important in her life. Sadly, both her mother and grandmother suffered from mental illness. She might have feared this in herself.

## *Mars*

- Mars (Assertiveness, Competition, Courage) in
- Taurus (Dependable, Idealistic, Practical) in the
- Tenth House (Achievement, Ambitious, Business Affairs, Infamy)
- Conjunction (Concentration, New Venture)
- Venus (Love, Female Relations, Love Affairs, Partner)
- Square (Accomplishment, Tension)
- Saturn (Achievement, Ambition, Bondage, Hard Work)
- Square (Accomplishment, Tension)
- Pluto (Movies, Sexuality)
- Conjunction (Concentration, New Venture)
- Midheaven (Achievement, Ambitious, Business Affairs, Infamy)
- Square (Accomplishment, Tension)
- Ascendant (Ambitions, Appearance, How Others See the Individual)

• Interpretation for Marilyn Monroe's Mars: Mars focuses on business, monetary accomplishment and security. She would do this through her beauty and sexuality as expressed through her movies, interviews, and TV appearances. But even she recognized that this focus on beauty and sexuality was a sacrifice to her own self, her own being.

## *Jupiter*

- Jupiter (Education, Good Fortune, Professional Ability) in
- Scorpio (Passionate, Resourceful, Sex) in the
- Fourth House (Family, Emotional Needs, Home)
- Conjunction (Concentration, New Venture)
- Moon (Emotional Needs, Family, Women)
- Opposition (Destructive)
- Venus (Love, Female Relations, Love Affairs, Partner)

• Interpretation for Marilyn Monroe's Jupiter: Jupiter in Marilyn Monroe's chart, like her Sun sign, emphasized good fortune in her professional life. It also reinforced that this helpless blond was not that helpless. According to the Keyword System, Marilyn had a natural business sense, a resourcefulness and a passion. If Marilyn had had access to the Keyword System she would no doubt have had more confidence in opening her own production company, Marilyn Monroe Productions in 1955. She boldly opened up her company and within a few months had negotiated more money and better working conditions for herself. One minute Marilyn was a star, strong, accomplished, running the show, the next she seemed so vulnerable. Pills and alcohol entered the scene. The Keyword System indicates that this was not just because of unhappy relations with men. Her instability goes far back. The Moon sign points to issues with women. Both her mother and her grandmother suffered from mental illness. It is not hard to guess that fear of her own mental illness may have over shadowed her life.

## Saturn

- Saturn (Achievement, Ambition, Bondage, Hard Work) in
- Leo (Dramatic, Generous, Optimistic) in the
- Twelfth House (Behind the scenes, Clandestine Affairs, Disappointments)
- Sextile (Affability, Attraction, Courage)
- Sun (Achievement, Acting, Creative Talent)
- Square (Accomplishment, Tension)
- Mars (Assertiveness, Competition)
- Sextile (Affability, Attraction)
- Neptune (Acting, Glamor, Orphanages)
- Conjunction (Concentration, New Venture)
- Pluto (Abuse, Betrayal, Sex)
- Square (Accomplishment, Tension)
- Midheaven (Achievement, Ambitious, Business Affairs, Infamy)
- Interpretation for Marilyn Monroe's Saturn: Marilyn Monroe was bound to work on her achievements but there was so much going on behind the scenes that complicated her life. She was always optimistic about her career which allowed her to progress in her acting career. There was so much that was unveiled after her death that was not known while she was alive.

We examine the keywords in other sections of the chart to gain additional information. Sometime all these areas are quite similar. A visit to YouTube will bring you face to face with stories that mix Marilyn up with the CIA and people high up in the government. These issues were kept secret as much as possible.

## Uranus

- Uranus (Movies, Deviation from the Norm, Infamy) in
- Gemini (Adaptable, Childlike, Intellectual, Talkative) in the
- Eleventh House (Idea of Happiness, Income from Business or Career, Receiving Love)
- Interpretation of Marilyn Monroe's Uranus: For a woman in Marilyn Monroe's time, she made a significant amount of money from her movies. This didn't come because the movie industry had a good heart and good intentions. It came because Marilyn had a sense for business.

## Neptune

- Neptune (Acting, Glamor, Orphanages) in
- Libra (Clothing Model, Persuasive, Sociable) in the
- Third House (Adaptability, Skill at Communication, Cleverness)
- Trine (Ease)
- Sun (Achievement, Acting, Creative Talent)
- Sextile (Affability, Attraction)

- Saturn (Achievement, Ambition, Bondage, Hard work)
- Sextile (Affability, Attraction)
- Pluto (Dreams and Visions, Sexuality, Movies)
- Sextile (Affability, Attraction)
- Ascendant (Ambitions, Appearance, How Others See the Individual)

• Interpretation of Marilyn Monroe's Neptune: Neptune focuses more on how people saw Marilyn. She started out modeling and was the subject of a nude calendar photographed in 1949: quite the scandal in those days. Most women would have been in the shadows after the calendar but her career soared. Why? She was beautiful but portrayed herself as a character, not taking herself and her sexuality seriously. She was cute, talkative, and often funny.

### Pluto

- Pluto (Dreams and Visions, Sexuality, Movies) in
- Leo (Dramatic, Generous, Optimistic) in the
- Twelfth House (Behind the Scenes, Clandestine Affairs, Disappointments)
- Square (Accomplishment, Tension)
- Moon (Emotional Needs, Family, Women)
- Sextile (Affability, Attraction)
- Sun (Achievement, Acting, Creative Talent)
- Square (Accomplishment, Tension)
- Venus (Love, Female Relations, Love Affairs, Partner)
- Square (Accomplishment, Tension)
- Mars (Assertiveness, Competition, Courage)
- Conjunction (Concentration, New Venture)
- Saturn (Achievement, Ambition, Bondage, Hard Work)
- Sextile (Affability, Attraction)
- Neptune (Acting, Glamor, Orphanages)
- Conjunction (Concentration, New Venture)
- Ascendant (Ambitions, Appearance, How Others See the Individual)

• Interpretation for Marilyn Monroe's Pluto: This planet duplicates other aspects and keywords, reinforcing that her life could have been pretty much predicted by this Keyword System. She struggled with the sexual assault issues she had as a child but used these difficulties to raise to fame and fortune.

It is obvious that Mother Teresa could not have lived Marilyn's life and Marilyn could not have lived Mother Teresa's life. Some of readers will probably enjoy doing what I did: take someone you know personally or who is famous and find the keywords that go with that chart.

## Horary Example: Will I Sell My Car?
- Mercury (Uranus secondary ruler) (car)
- Mercury in Libra retrograde (indecisive)
- In the ninth house (person at a distance)
- Mercury (car) opposition (destructive) Moon (female)

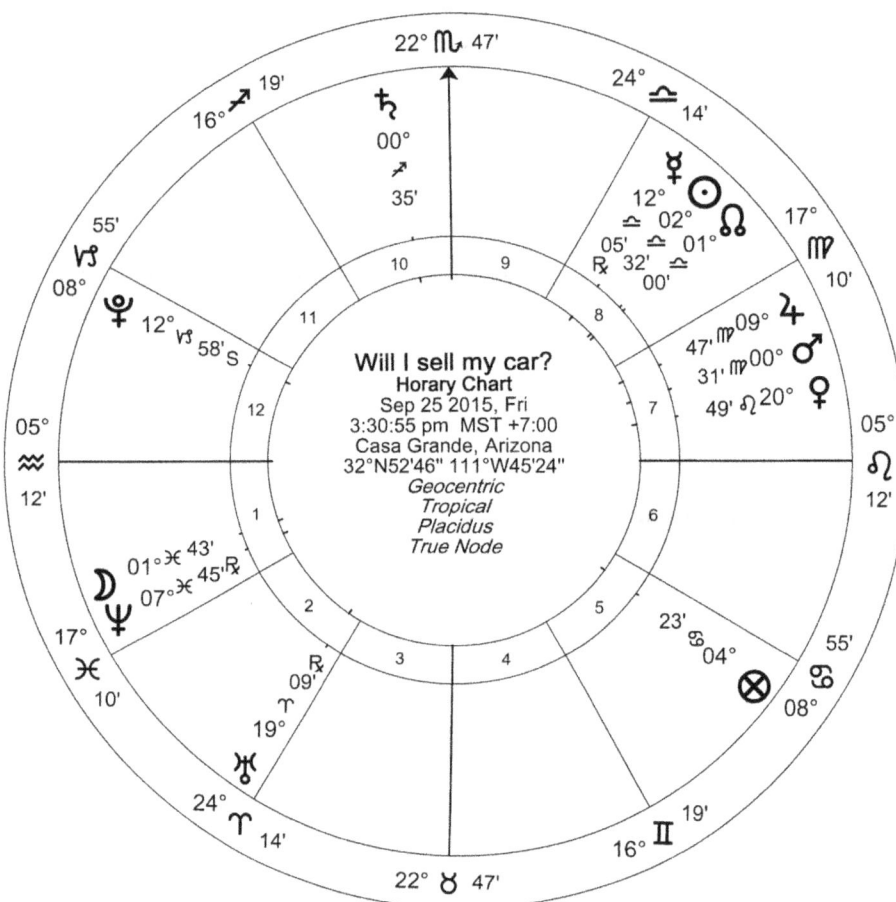

- Mercury (car) opposition (destructive) Jupiter (good fortune)

The person at a distance is indecisive and is at a disadvantage regarding buying the car. She is a female.

- Uranus (retrograde, not fully functional) (car) in the sixth house (owner is an accountant).
- Maybe there is something not right with the car.
- Uranus (retrograde, not fully functional) (car) conjunction (union) Moon (woman) separating
- Uranus (retrograde, not fully functional) (car) quincux (redirecting) Venus (money) Uranus (retrograde, not fully functional) (car) conjunction (union) Jupiter (fairness) Uranus (retrograde, not fully functional) (car) square (tension) Uranus (electrical)

Again, is there something wrong with the car? Yes, there was something wrong with the car. And what is a fair price?

- Uranus (retrograde, not fully functional) (electrical) opposition Neptune (phone)
- The electrical issue was not revealed during the phone calls.
- Uranus (retrograde, not fully functional) (car) trine (ease) Pluto (secrets about the electricity)

The selling of the car is causing the owner (Ascendant) some nervousness.

The question was asked in order to determine if it would sell and for how much. With all this, it doesn't look good, does it? I'd say that the querent probably, depending on the rest of the chart, will not get what he wants for the car. If the purchaser is a female, she is at a disadvantage. The car was sold after a dramatic decrease in the price. And it was sold to a female.

Following is a brief interpretation of the horary chart:

The ruler of automobiles is Mercury, which is in the eighth house of debts, and in Libra, which indicates indecisiveness. The seller may want too much, setting the price according to the debts he wants to pay off rather than the value of the car.

Another ruler of automobiles is Uranus, which is retrograde and in the second house. This indicates that the value of the vehicle is misplaced. In Aries, there could be a lack of follow-through, so the car might not be listed again—at least not now, if the price isn't lowered.

In horary charts the Moon indicates the time frame of anything that will happen related to the question. The Moon in the first of the Querent is sextile (attraction) Pluto (endings).

The Moon is in an angular house and in a mutable sign, indicating that the activities will happen in 11 days, weeks, months, or years, according to the following:

|          | *Angular* | *Succeedent* | *Cadent* |
|----------|-----------|--------------|----------|
| Cardinal | Day       | Weeks        | Months   |
| *Mutable*  | Weeks     | Months       | Years    |
| *Fixed*    | Months    | Years        | ?        |

I agree with Ivy M. Goldstein-Jacobson, author of *Simplified Horary Astrology*, that you need to adjust the time according to the believability of the chart. So the Moon will sextile Pluto in 11 days or weeks (depending on when reality sets in). In the end the seller drastically lowered the price after hearing the reading of the chart. The car was purchased by a woman who was so unsure she had her brother do all the work regarding the purchase of the car. The commitment to purchase was made 11 days after the car was listed. The purchaser lived some distance from the seller.

# A to Z Keywords

# A

AIDS
  8, Mars, Pluto
Abandoned houses
  Scorpio
Abdomen
  6, Mercury, Virgo
Ability as agent/speaker/teacher
  Mercury
Ability to handle funds
  2, Venus
Abnormal person
  Neptune
Abortion, spontaneous
  5, Uranus
Abortion, surgical
  8, Mars, Pluto
Abrasion
  8, 6, Mars
Abrasive
  Sesquisquare
Abscess
  Moon, Taurus
Abstract Thinking
  9
Abstraction
  9, Jupiter
Abuse
  8, Pluto
Abyss
  Pluto
Academia
  9, Jupiter
Academic Aims
  9
Academic Subjects
  9, Jupiter
Academic success
  Jupiter
Acceptance
  12, Pisces
Accidents
  1, 3, Gemini, Mercury, Mars, Uranus

Accident to throat or neck
  Taurus
Accident, liability
  1, 9, Mars
Accommodation
  4, Moon
Accomplice
  Pluto
Accomplishment
  Square
Accounts
  8, 6, Mercury, Virgo
Accuracy
  3, Mercury
Achievement
  10, Saturn, Sun
Acne
  Aries
Acquaintances
  11, Uranus
Acquaintance, New
  11
Acquiring
  Taurus
Acting
  5, Neptune, Sun, Venus
Action
  1, Mars
Action that affects health
  6
Active head of an enterprise
  10, Sun
Activity
  1, Mars, Aries
Activity, new
  Conjunction, parallel
Actor
  5, Venus, Neptune, Leo
Acute fever
  Sun, Mars, Aries
Ad writer
  3, Mercury
Adaptability
  3, Mercury

Adaptable
  Gemini
Addict
  12, Neptune
Adjustment
  Inconjunct
Administration
  10, Sun
Administrator
  10, Saturn, Sun
Administrator, estate
  Capricorn
Adolescence
  Venus
Adopted child
  Aquarius
Adoption
  Aquarius
Adornment
  5, Sun, Venus
Adrenal gland
  Libra, Aries
Adultery
  5, Venus
Advanced degrees
  9, 12, Jupiter
Advanced thinking
  Uranus
Advancement
  10, Sun
Advancement, economic
  2, Venus , Jupiter
Adventurers
  1, Mars
Adversaries
  7
Advertisement (written copy)
  3, Mercury
Advertisers
  3, Mercury
Advertising
  9, Sun, Jupiter
Advertising department
  9

*Astrological Keywords*

Advisor, Personal
  7
Advisors as a class
  11, Uranus
Aesthetics
  Venus
Affability
  Sextile
Affairs of an in-law
  9
Affairs of late life
  4
Affairs of an official
  10
Affairs of a parent
  4, 10
Affairs of the heart
  5, Venus
Affection
  5, Venus
Affectionate Matters
  Venus
Affiliation in a group
  11, Uranus
Affliction
  12
Affluence
  Jupiter
Afghanistan
  Saturn
Afraid
  Aquarius
Africa, North and West
  Cancer
Agate stone
  Mercury, Saturn, Gemini, Virgo
Age
  Saturn
Agency
  6, Mercury
Agent
  3, 6, Mercury, Virgo
Agent of the querent
  7
Agent of justice
  9
Agent, secret
  Pluto

Aggression
  Mars, Leo
Aggressors
  1, Mars
Aging
  Saturn
Agitation
  Sesquisquare
Agitation
  Sesquisquare, Uranus
Agreement
  7, Venus
Agreement (written document)
  3, Mercury
Agriculture
  Ceres
Agriculture
  4, Saturn, Moon
Agricultural product
  4
Air conditioning
  6, Uranus, Saturn
Air conditioning unit
  Aquarius
Airline
  Aquarius
Aircraft
  9, Uranus, Gemini, Aquarius
Airplane
  Uranus, Aquarius
Airport
  9
Alarm
  Uranus
Alabaster stone
  Venus, Taurus, Libra
Albania
  Capricorn
Alchemy
  8, Pluto
Alcohol
  Neptune
Alcohol, those whose work is
    connected with
  Neptune
Alcoholic
  Pluto
Alcoholism
  12, Moon, Neptune, Pluto

Alderman
  11
Ale Houses
  5
Alfalfa
  Virgo
Algeria
  Scorpio
Aliens
  9
Alimentary canal
  Virgo
Alimentary system
  Cancer
Alimony
  8
Allergic substances
  Moon
Allergy
  6, Cancer, Uranus
Allergy, food
  Virgo
Alliances
  7, Venus
Ally
  7, Libra
Almond tree
  Venus
Almond
  Jupiter, Taurus
Alps
  Leo
Alteration
  8
Altruism
  9, 11, 12, Jupiter
Altruistic
  Aquarius
Altruistic undertaking
  9, 11
Aluminum metal
  Aquarius
Amateur in pursuit of love
  Leo
Ambassador
  5, Moon, Mercury, Leo
Amber stone
  Sun, Uranus

Ambition
  10, Sun, Saturn
Ambitions
  11
Ambitious
  Leo
Ambush
  12, Pluto
Amethyst (stone)
  Jupiter, Neptune, Aries,
  Sagittarius, Pluto
Ammunition of a besieged town
  5
Amnesia
  Pluto
Amphibious creature
  Cancer
Amsterdam
  Cancer
Amusement park
  5, Sun
Amusement, owners of a place of
  Leo
Amusement
  5, Venus, Sun
Analysis
  8, Mercury, Pluto
Anarchist
  Pluto
Anarchy
  Pluto
Ancestor
  2, 4, Saturn
Ancient dwelling
  4
Ancient matters
  Saturn
Anemia
  Neptune, Gemini
Anesthetic
  Neptune
Angelica herb
  Sun, Leo
Anger
  Mars
Angina Pectoris
  Leo
Animal husbandry
  6

Animal stables
  Aries
Animal
  5
Animal as pet
  6, Aries
Animal beyond control
  Virgo
Animals in a zoo
  12
Animals, fondness for
  12
Animal, wild
  Jupiter
Animal, large
  12
Animal, missing
  12, Jupiter, Leo
Animal, newborn
  Moon
Animals, Small
  Cancer
Animal, small domesticated
  6
Animal, caring for
  Ceres
Animal, threatening
  12
Aniseed herb
  Mercury, Gemini
Ankle
  11, Uranus, Aquarius
Ankle, sprained or broken
  Aquarius
Annoyance
  Mercury
Annuity
  Scorpio
Anonymity
  Pluto
Anonymous letter
  Mercury
Antibiotics
  6
Antique
  4, Moon, Uranus, Aquarius
Antique collector
  Aquarians

Antiseptic
  Neptune
Ant
  Mercury, Pluto
Antwerp
  Libra
Anus
  Scorpio
Anxious
  Virgo
Anyone unrelated by blood
  7
Anyone who is a stranger
  5
Anything created by Querent
  7, 9, Jupiter
Anything electronic
  Uranus
Anything hidden in the ground
  4
Appearance
  1
Appraising
  Capricorn
Artistic
  Leo
Artistic output
  5
Ascetics
  Neptune
Ashram
  12
Asia Minor
  Taurus
Asparagus
  Jupiter, Libra, Sagittarius
Aspirations
  11, Jupiter
Assassin
  12
Assassination
  12, Neptune
Assembly
  Aquarius
Assertion
  Mars
Assertiveness
  Mars

Astrological Keywords

Asset, liquid or monetary
: 2, Venus, Part of Fortune

Assets, negotiable
: 2

Asset, tangible
: 2, Venus

Assimilation
: Moon

Associate
: 7, 11, Uranus

Asthma
: Mercury, Gemini, Cancer

Astral experience
: 8

Astrologer
: Uranus

Astrological affairs
: 11, Uranus

Astrological counselor
: 7, Uranus

Astrology
: 9, Uranus

Astrology, horary
: 9, Neptune, Jupiter, Uranus

Astronaut
: Aquarius

Astronomer
: Aquarius

Astronomy
: Uranus, Aquarius

Asylum
: 12

Athlete
: Mars, Sagittarius

Athletic coach
: Leo

Athletic contest
: 5, 7, Mars

Athletic sport for show or gain
: 5, Sun

Atom
: Sun

Atomic bomb
: Pluto

Atomic energy
: Pluto

Atomic power
: Pluto

Atomic scientist
: Pluto

Atrophy
: Saturn

Attainment
: 10, Saturn, Sun

Attic
: 9, Jupiter, Libra

Attitude toward God
: 9

Attorney
: 9

Attraction
: Sextile

Auction
: 10

Audit, tax or financial
: 8

Aunt, paternal
: 12

Aunt, maternal
: 6

Aunts and uncles (generic)
: 6

Aunt, illness of
: 5

Aura
: Uranus

Australia
: Sagittarius

Austria
: Libra

Authority
: 10, Sun, Sagittarius

Author
: Mercury

Autocratic
: Leo

Automobile
: 3, Mercury, Uranus, Mars

Autonomy
: Uranus

Aviation
: Taurus

Avocado
: Uranus, Aquarius

Avocation
: 5

Awakener, the
: Uranus

Award
: 10, Uranus

Aware
: Scorpio

Awareness
: 5, Mercury, Opposition

# B

Baby
: 5, Moon

Baby shower
: 5

Babysitter
: Moon

Back, anatomy
: 5, Sun

Back, lower
: 7, Venus, Libra

Back, upper
: 5, Sun, Libra

Back weakness
: Libra

Back wound
: Leo

Backache
: Libra

Bacteria
: Neptune, Pluto

Bad Habit
: 12

Baghdad
: Virgo

Bail bond
: 8

Bail, get out on
: 12, Jupiter

Bailiff
: Mars

Baker
: Moon

Balance
: 7, Venus, Opposition

Balcony
: Jupiter, Sagittarius, Aquarius

Ballet
: Neptune, Pluto

Ballet dancer
: Neptune

Balloon
: Aquarius

Balm herb
: Cancer, Mercury, Gemini

Banana
: Taurus

Band leader
: Aries

Banished person
: 7, 12

Bank account
: 2

Banker
: 2, Venus, Jupiter, Taurus

Bankrupt
: 8, Saturn, Neptune

Bank
: Venus

Baptize
: Moon

Barbary Coast
: Scorpio

Barber
: Mercury

Barley
: Saturn

Barn for farm machinery
: Capricorn

Barn, airy
: Gemini

Barn, dairy
: Taurus

Barracuda
: Scorpio

Barren land
: Aries

Bar (tavern)
: 5, Cancer

Bartender
: Cancer

Base of operations
: 4

Basement
: 4, Saturn, Taurus

Basic, bare bones
: 8

Basic utilities
: 4, Moon

Basic security
: Saturn

Basil herb
: Mars, Scorpio

Bath
: Neptune

Bathing
: Moon

Bathroom
: 8, Cancer

Battery
: Uranus

Battle
: 7, Mars

Bavarian
: Scorpio

Bay tree
: Jupiter, Sagittarius

Bay herb
: Sun

Beach
: 4, Moon, Neptune, Cancer

Beam (wooden)
: Saturn

Bean
: Taurus, Aquarius

Bear
: Saturn

Beast, wild
: Leo

Beautician
: Venus

Beautification
: Venus, Neptune

Beauty
: Venus

Beauty parlor
: Libra

Beauty, thing of
: 7, Venus

Bed
: Venus

Bedroom
: 5, 8, Venus

Beekeeper
    Leo
Bee
    Mercury
Beggar
    12, Saturn
Beginning of an enterprise
    1
Beginning of life
    Pluto
Beginnings and endings
    1
Beginning, new
    1, 8, Mars, Pluto
Beheading
    Taurus
Behavior, unique
    Chiron
Behind the scenes
    12
Belfry
    Aquarius
Belgium
    Gemini
Belief system
    9, Jupiter
Belief, secret
    4
Belongings
    2
Beloved pet
    5, Venus
Belt
    Capricorn
Beneath the ground
    4
Bergamot herb
    Pisces
Berlin
    Aquarius
Berry
    Jupiter
Beryl stone
    Venus, Gemini, Libra, Neptune
Betrayal
    Pluto, Neptune
Bet and betting
    5

Beverage
    Moon, Neptune
Bible
    Jupiter
Bicycle
    3, Uranus, Gemini
Big picture
    10
Bigamist
    Neptune
Bigot
    Saturn
Bilberry herb
    Jupiter
Bill
    8, 2
Binding
    Saturn, conjunction, parallel
Binds, anything that
    Saturn
Bingo
    5
Birch tree
    Jupiter
Bird, fancy plumage
    6
Bird, song
    Mercury
Bird, wild
    Leo
Bird, as Pet
    9
Bird, carrier pigeon
    Saturn, Scorpio
Bird in flight
    Gemini
Bird of prey
    Taurus
Bird, small
    Mercury
Bird, talking
    Cancer
Bird, water
    12
Birth
    8, 1, Moon, Pluto
Birth Control
    8

Birth defect due to drug use
    Pluto
Birth Deformity
    Pluto
Birth rate
    5
Birth, injury due to delivery
    Pluto
Bisexuality
    Neptune
Bishop
    9
Blackcurrant herb
    Taurus
Blackmail
    12, Neptune
Blackness
    Saturn
Blacksmith
    Mars, Aries
Bladder
    8, Mars, Pluto, Scorpio
Bladder Disorder
    Mars, Pluto, Venus, Scorpio
Blasphemy
    12
Bleeding, excessive
    Aries
Blessing
    Jupiter
Blister
    Mars
Blood
    Jupiter
Blood clot
    Venus
Blood disease
    Mars, Jupiter
Blood poisoning
    Aquarius
Blood circulation
    Mars
Blood, impure
    Venus, Jupiter, Uranus, Aquarius
Blood pressure, high
    Taurus, Gemini
Blood, venous
    Jupiter

Bloodshed
  Venus
Bloodstain
  Aries
Bloodstone stone
  Mars, Aries, Scorpio, Uranus
Blow inflicted by force
  Mars, Pluto, Saturn
Blunt
  Sagittarius
Blunt instrument
  Saturn
Board of directors
  6
Boarder or tenant
  Mars, Aries
Boarding house
  4
Boasting
  11, 5
Boat
  5, Sun, Leo
Boat, small
  Cancer
Bodily well-being
  Moon
Body
  1, 6
Body of a vehicle
  1
Body fluid
  Moon
Body, sides of
  1
Bohemia
  Leo
Bohemian
  Leo
Boil
  Uranus
Bomb
  Jupiter, Aries
Bondage
  Uranus, Pluto
Bondage, those in
  12, Saturn, Pluto
Bonding with others
  Pluto

Bond
  7, Venus
Bone surgeon
  2, Jupiter
Bone
  2, Jupiter
Bone, broken
  Capricorn
Book worm
  10, Saturn
Bookkeeper
  Capricorn
Bookkeeping office
  Gemini
Book
  6, Mercury, Virgo
Book, account
  Virgo
Book, old
  9, 3, Mercury, Gemini
Bookshelf
  Virgo
Boots
  Aquarius
Borage herb
  Mercury
Border, across the
  Mars
Border between countries or states
  9
Bored by details
  Capricorn
Bosnia
  Aquarius
Boss
  Capricorn
Botanist
  10, Sun, Saturn
Boundary
  Venus
Bowel, lower
  Saturn, Capricorn
Bowel movement
  8
Bowel, upper
  Pluto, Scorpio
Bowels
  Virgo

Boxer
  Leo
Box
  3, 6, Mercury, Gemini
Brain
  1, Moon, Mercury, Mars, Sun, Aries
Brain matter
  Moon
Brass metal
  Venus
Brazil
  Virgo
Breakage
  Mars
Breaking Free
  Uranus
Break
  Uranus
Breast cancer
  Cancer
Breast
  Moon, Cancer
Breathing
  3, Mercury
Bremen
  Aquarius
Brewer
  Moon
Brewing
  Moon
Bribery
  8, 12, Neptune
Brick layer
  Saturn, Capricorn
Brick
  Saturn
Bridge, high
  Sagittarius
Bring to justice
  Saturn
Broadcast
  Uranus
Broadcaster
  Sagittarius
Broadcasting, commercial
  Sagittarius
Broad-minded
  Sagittarius

Astrological Keywords

Broccoli
    Aries, Aquarius
Brokerage
    Mercury
Broker
    Jupiter
Bronchitis
    Mercury, Gemini, Cancer
Bronze
    Venus, Taurus
Bronze, object made of
    Taurus
Brooding
    Saturn, Capricorn, Cancer
Brook
    Cancer
Brothel owner
    8, Scorpio
Brother-in-law
    9
Brother
    3, Mercury
Brother, younger
    Jupiter
Brusque
    Aries
Brutality
    8, Pluto, Mars
Budapest
    Scorpio
Budget
    2, Venus
Builder
    4, Saturn
Building
    4
Building, commercial
    Capricorn
Building, condemned
    Pluto
Building, functional
    Capricorn
Buildings, government
    Leo
Bulgaria
    Capricorn
Bull ring
    Taurus

Bunion
    Pluto
Burglar
    7, 12, Mars
Burglary
    12
Burial
    4
Burma
    Libra
Burning
    Mars
Burn
    Mars, Sagittarius
Bus driver
    3, Mercury
Bus boy
    6
Bus
    3, Mercury, Jupiter, Gemini
Business
    7, 10, Scorpio, Capricorn
Business, accounting
    8
Business affairs
    10
Business asset
    11
Business associate
    7
Business dealings abroad
    9
Business deal, big
    Uranus
Business income
    11
Business manager
    Capricorn
Business or professional standing
    10
Business partner
    7
Business person
    Mercury, Saturn
Business success
    10
Business world
    10

Business, big
    10
Business, place of
    10
Businesslike
    Capricorn
Businessperson (big business)
    Jupiter
Busybody
    Mercury
Butcher
    8, Mars, Pluto, Scorpio
Butcher shop
    Scorpio
Butler
    6
Buttocks
    7, Jupiter, Sagittarius
Buyer
    7
Buying
    7

# C

C.I.A.
 Pluto
Cabbage
 Moon, Cancer
Cabinet maker
 Libra
Cabinet
 Virgo
Cactus
 Mars
Cadaver
 8
Cafeteria
 4, 6, Moon, Mercury
Calamint
 Mercury
Calamity
 Saturn
Calcium deficiency disease
 Capricorn
Calendar
 Saturn
Calf
 Venus
Calm things down
 Venus
Calf (leg)
 Uranus, Aquarius
Camera
 3, Mercury, Neptune
Camouflage
 Neptune
Camphor herb
 Saturn, Capricorn
Canal
 Moon, Cancer
Cancer
 Moon, Pisces
Cancer of breast, stomach, uterus
 Cancer
Candid
 Sagittarius
Candy
 Venus

Capillary
 Gemini
Capitalism
 Jupiter
Captivity
 12
Car
 3, Mercury, Mars, Uranus, Gemini
Car repair
 3, Mercury
Car, used car salespeople
 12
Caraway herb
 Mercury, Gemini
Carbon
 Saturn
Carbuncle (stone)
 Sun, Jupiter, Leo, Virgo, Sagittarius
Cardiac status
 Sun
Cards, game
 5
Cards, playing
 Gemini
Care of pet
 6
Career
 10
Career activities
 10
Career of children
 2
Career of partner
 4
Career, capacity for
 Saturn
Career, money from
 11
Careful
 6, Virgo
Caretaker
 6, Moon, Cancer

Carnelian stone
 Uranus, Libra
Caring for
 6
Carpenter
 Mars, Libra
Carrot
 Mercury, Gemini, Capricorn
Cash in hand
 2, Venus, Part of Fortune
Cash Flow
 2, Venus
Cash register
 2, Venus
Cask, wooden
 Capricorn
Caspian Sea, areas near
 Libra
Castle
 4, Cancer, Leo
Castration
 Uranus, Scorpio
Casualties, with others
 11
Catalepsy
 Neptune
Catalonia, Spain
 Scorpio
Cataract
 Sun
Categorization
 6, Mercury
Caterer
 Moon
Cathedral
 Sagittarius
Cat
 6, Venus, Mercury, Virgo
Cattle
 Venus, Taurus
Cattle, large
 12
Cattle breeder
 Taurus

Cattle market
    Venus
Cattle rancher
    4, Venus
Cauliflower
    Moon, Gemini, Leo, Scorpio
Cause of event
    11
Caution
    Saturn
Cautious
    Capricorn
Cautious, overly
    Cancer
Cave
    Cancer, Saturn
Cayenne herb
    Mars, Aries
Ceiling
    Aries
Ceiling, close to
    Sagittarius
Ceiling and plastered walls
    Aries
Celebration, as festival
    5, 11, Sun
Celibacy
    6
Celibate
    Scorpio
Cellar
    Taurus, Saturn
Cellar, underground
    Cancer
Cement
    Saturn
Cement worker
    Capricorn
Cemetery
    4, 8, Saturn
Cemetery plot
    4, Moon
Cemetery worker
    Mars
Ceramics
    Saturn
Cereal
    Pluto

Cerebellum
    Taurus
Cerebral congestion
    Aries
Cerebral hemorrhage
    Aries
Cerebrum
    Aries
Ceremony
    5, 9
Ceremony as a group function
    11
Ceremony that legalizes a matter
    9, Jupiter
Cervical vertebrae
    Taurus
Cesarean
    Uranus, Scorpio
Cesspool
    8
Chains
    Saturn, Capricorn
Chairman of the board
    10, Saturn
Chakra
    Neptune
Chakra, first, red
    Mars
Chakra, second, orange
    Jupiter
Chakra, third, yellow
    Moon
Chakra, fourth, green
    Sun
Chakra, fifth, blue
    Neptune
Chakra, seventh, violet
    Pluto
Chalcedony stone
    Aquarius
Challenge
    Square
Challenger in a contest
    7
Challenges one tries to overcome
    South Node
Chamber of Commerce
    11

Chamomile herb
    Sun
Chance
    5
Chance, operations of the law
    5
Chance, things that depend on
    5
Change
    8, Moon
Change of locale
    7
Change, quick
    Gemini, Uranus
Change, slow
    Taurus
Changeable
    Gemini
Changing conditions
    Moon
Change
    Moon
Chaos
    Neptune
Chapel
    9
Character defect
    12, Neptune
Charge account
    8
Charge card
    8
Charitable
    Pisces
Charitable act
    12
Charitable institution
    12, Neptune, Jupiter
Charitable organization that
    feeds people
    Cancer
Charity
    12, Neptune, Jupiter
Charity given and received
    12, Neptune, Jupiter
Charity organizer
    Cancer
Charleston, South Carolina
    Libra

Charm
  Venus
Chattel
  2
Cheat
  Neptune
Checkbook
  2, Venus
Checking account
  2, Venus
Check
  Mercury
Cheerfulness
  Venus
Cheese
  Moon, Gemini, Leo, Virgo,
  Aquarius
Chef
  Moon
Chemical warfare
  Neptune
Chemicals
  Neptune, Pluto, Pisces
Chemistry
  Neptune
Chemist
  6, Mars, Neptune, Pisces
Chemists, organic
  Cancer
Chess
  Gemini
Chest (high)
  Gemini
Chest top
  Libra
Chicago
  Leo
Chicken
  6, Moon
Chicory herb
  Jupiter
Chief executive
  10, Saturn, Sun
Child
  5, Leo
Child, adopted
  11, 5, Aquarius
Child, biological
  5

Child, conception of
  4, 5, Moon
Children, dealing with
  5
Child, death of
  12
Child, female
  Moon
Child, male
  Sun
Child, out of wedlock
  Neptune, Pisces
Child, legitimacy of
  5
Child of another
  11
Child-in-law
  11
Child querent
  Leo
Child, step
  11
Child's affairs
  5
Child's brain
  5
Childbirth
  5, Moon, Cancer
Childhood disease
  Cancer
Childhood environment
  1
Childhood, early
  1
Childish
  Leo
Childlike
  Gemini
Chimney sweeper
  Saturn
Chimney
  Mars, Taurus, Leo
China
  Libra
China ware
  Moon
Chiropractor
  Saturn

Choir
  Venus, Taurus
Choking
  Saturn, Taurus, Neptune
Cholera
  Leo, Virgo
Christianity
  Neptune, Pluto
Chronic illness
  12, Saturn
Chronic invalid
  Capricorn
Chrysolite stone
  Venus, Taurus, Libra, Pisces
Church
  9, Jupiter
Church affiliation
  9
Church matters
  9
Churchmen
  9, Jupiter
Cinema as entertainment
  5
Cinnamon
  Sun
Circulation of blood
  Venus, Uranus, Aquarius
Circulation, poor
  Leo
Circulation, stoppage of blood
  Venus, Saturn
Circulatory disorder
  Aquarius
Circulatory system
  Sun, Jupiter, Uranus
Circumstance beyond the
  querent's control
  11
Circumstantial development
  11
Circus performer
  Leo
Circus
  Leo
Cistern
  Cancer
City
  4

Citrus tree
  Sun
City Council
  11
City official
  10
City engineer
  Mercury
Civil lawyer
  Saturn
Civil rights
  Aquarius
Civil servant
  Saturn
Civil service
  6, Saturn, Virgo
Civil service worker
  6
Clairvoyance
  10, 12, Neptune, Uranus
Clairvoyant
  Pisces
Clam
  Moon, Scorpio, Neptune
Clan
  4
Clandestine
  Neptune
Clandestine affair
  12, Neptune
Clandestine associate
  12
Clandestine work
  12
Claw
  7, Venus
Clean
  Virgo
Cleaner
  Moon
Cleaning out
  8, Pluto
Clearheaded
  Capricorn
Clearing away
  8, Pluto
Clergy
  9, Jupiter, Sagittarius

Clergyperson
  Jupiter
Clerical work
  Mercury
Clerking
  Mercury
Clerk
  3, 6, Mercury
Cleaver
  Gemini
Cleverness
  3, Mercury
Client
  6, Mercury
Climate
  6
Client
  6, Mercury
Climate
  6
Clinic
  6, 12
Clockmaker
  Virgo
Clock
  Saturn, Uranus
Close relative
  3, Mercury
Closet
  Moon, Virgo
Clothing as possession
  2
Clothing as vanity
  5
Clothing model
  Libra
Clothing, evening
  Venus
Clothing, fashionable
  Libra
Clothing in general
  6, Mercury
Clothing, useful
  6
Cloudiness
  Neptune
Clouds
  Aquarius

Clover
  Virgo
Clown costume
  Saturn
Clown
  Sagittarius, Scorpio, Aquarius
Club house
  Aquarius
Club house for public meeting
  Aquarius
Club member
  11
Club
  11
Club as an instrument
  Saturn
Club, social
  Venus
Clumsy
  Taurus
Coach, athletic
  Leo
Coagulate
  Saturn
Coal
  Saturn, Capricorn
Coal miner
  Capricorn
Coccygeal vertebrae
  Sagittarius
Cockroach
  Pluto
Cocktail party
  5
Code of ethics
  9, Jupiter
Coercion
  Pluto
Coffee
  Mars
Coffin
  Saturn
Cohabitation prompted by love
  7
Coin
  2, Venus
Cold
  Taurus, Saturn

Cold temperament
    Aquarius, Saturn
Coldest part of the house
    Saturn
Coldness
    Saturn
Collarbone
    3
Collection
    Moon
Collector of antiques
    Aquarius
College
    9, Jupiter
Cologne, city of
    Sagittarius
Colon
    Scorpio
Color
    Venus
Color, aqua
    Moon
Color, ashen
    Jupiter
Color, azure blue
    Venus, Mercury
Color, black
    Saturn, Capricorn
Color, blue
    Mercury, Jupiter, Sagittarius,
    Pluto, Taurus, Virgo, Pisces
Color, blue crystal
    Gemini
Color, blue green
    Cancer
Color, blue violet
    Jupiter, Capricorn
Color, brown
    Taurus, Scorpio
Color, chartreuse
    Sagittarius
Color, checked
    Mercury, Uranus
Color, coral
    Libra
Color, cream
    Taurus
Color, crimson
    Libra
Color, dark brown
    Saturn
Color, deep blue
    Venus
Color, drab brown
    Mars
Color, electric blue
    Uranus
Color, gold
    Leo
Color, gray
    Capricorn
Color, gray-green
    Pisces
Color, green
    Moon, Cancer, Libra, Pisces
Color, greenish blue
    Scorpio
Color, honey
    5
Color, indigo
    Saturn, Capricorn, Aquarius
Color, iridescent
    Neptune
Color, lavender
    Neptune
Color, magenta
    Jupiter
Color, mauve
    Neptune
Color, mixed or streaked
    Uranus
Color, multicolored or plaid
    Uranus
Color, orange
    Sun, Gemini, Leo
Color, orange-yellow
    Cancer
Color, pale blue
    Venus
Color, pale green
    Moon
Color, pale yellowish white
    Moon
Color, pastel
    Venus, Libra
Color, piebald
    Gemini
Color, purple
    Mars, Jupiter
Color, red
    Mars, Taurus, Leo, Sagittarius
Color, murky red
    Scorpio
Color, red-orange
    Taurus
Color, saffron
    11, Sun
Color, sandy
    Sun
Color, Scarlet
    Mars
Color, sea-green
    Neptune
Color, silver
    Moon
Color, slate
    Mercury
Color, somber
    Capricorn
Color, spotted
    Jupiter
Color, violet
    Venus, Jupiter, Gemini, Virgo,
    Aquarius
Color, violet-red
    Pisces
Color, white
    1, 5, 9, 10, Moon, Neptune,
    Libra, Pluto
Color, wine
    Jupiter
Color, yellow
    3, 11, Sun, Taurus
Color, yellow-green
    Jupiter, Virgo, Sagittarius
Coma
    Neptune
Combat
    7, Mars
Comedian
    Gemini
Comet
    9
Comfort
    Venus

Comforts like food and clothing
 6
Comfrey herb
 Saturn, Capricorn
Comfort, where one provides
 Ceres
Comings and goings
 3, Mercury
Commander-in-chief
 10
Commander
 Sun
Commerce
 Moon
Commercial broadcasting
 Sagittarius
Commercial building
 Capricorn
Commission
 Uranus
Commitment to work
 Vesta
Commitment
 7
Committee of a fraternal group
 11
Commodities
 6, Moon, Mercury, Venus
Commodity exchange
 11
Common touch
 Moon
Commoner
 Uranus
Communication
 3, Mercury, Gemini
Communication over long distance
 9
Communication, one way
 Uranus
Communication, skill at
 3, Mercury
Communism
 Neptune
Community
 4, 11
Community affairs
 4, 11

Community minded
 Aquarius
Community weather
 4
Community property
 5, 8
Community resources
 5
Commuter
 , Mercury
Commuting
 3, Mercury, Gemini
Companionable
 Libra
Companionship
 Venus
Compass
 Jupiter
Compassion
 12, Neptune
Compassionate
 Pisces, Virgo
Compelling forces
 8, Pluto
Competing
 Lilith
Competition
 5, 7, Sun, Venus, Mars
Competitive
 Aries
Competitor
 7
Complicate
 Pluto
Compost Heap
 Capricorn
Compressed form
 Saturn
Compromise
 7, Venus
Compulsion
 8, Pluto
Compulsive sex
 8, Pluto
Compulsory cooperation
 Pluto
Computer operation
 Uranus

Computer programmer
 6, Virgo
Computer technician
 3, Uranus, Mercury
Computer
 3, Uranus, Mercury, Virgo
Con artist
 Neptune
Concave or wavy object
 Moon
Conceit
 Sun
Concentration
 Conjunction, Saturn
Concentration camp
 12, Neptune, Pisces
Concentration, lack of
 Gemini
Conception
 Pluto
Conceptual framework
 9, Jupiter
Concern (worry)
 Virgo
Concern for others
 12, Neptune
Concert
 5, Venus
Concrete structure
 10, Saturn
Conditions at close of life
 4
Confectionery
 Venus
Conference, large meeting
 9, 3, Mercury
Confidence
 11, North Node, Leo
Confidence, added
 North Node
Confidential information
 12, Neptune
Confidential activity
 12
Confidential agent
 12
Confidential matter
 12, Neptune

Confinement, any type of
    12
Confine and protect
    Capricorn
Confines, anything that
    Capricorn
Conflict
    Opposition
Confusion
    Neptune
Congenial
    Gemini, Venus
Congress
    11, Uranus
Connecting
    3, Gemini
Conquest
    Mars
Consciousness
    Sun
Consequences, remote
    4
Conservation
    6, Saturn, Virgo
Conservatism
    Saturn
Conservative
    Taurus
Conservative people
    Saturn
Conspiracy
    12, Neptune
Constantinople
    Cancer
Constipation
    Pluto, Saturn, Virgo
Construction
    Mars
Consultants, personal
    7
Consultation from an expert
    7
Consummation
    Venus
Contest
    7
Conversation
    Gemini

Cool
    Capricorn
Co-op
    Aquarius
Co-worker
    11
Court, probate
    Capricorn
Courtship
    5, Venus
Cousin, generic
    3, Mercury
Cousin, maternal
    4
Cousin, paternal
    10
Convent
    7
Covert
    Pluto
Cowboy
    Taurus
Coworker
    6, Mercury
Crab
    Moon
Crafts
    6
Craftsmanship
    6
Craftsman
    6, Mercury
Cramps
    Uranus, Capricorn
Cramp, leg
    Aquarius
Crank, crackpot
    Uranus
Creative
    5, Leo
Creative activity
    5
Creative energy
    Sun
Creative manipulation of ideas
    9
Creative talent
    5, Sun, Venus

Creative work
    5
Creative writing
    5, Sun
Creativity
    5, Sun
Creature, dangerous sea
    Scorpio
Credit
    8, 10, Sun
Credit union
    8, 6
Crematory
    8, Mars, Pluto
Crete
    Virgo
Crime
    8, 12, Pluto, Neptune
Criminal action
    Pluto
Criminal hangout
    Pisces
Criminal lawyer
    Libra
Criminal
    12, Aries
Criminal at large
    7
Criminal on trial
    7
Criminals, one who works with
    Neptune
Critical
    Virgo
Criticism
    8
Criticism, friendly
    11
Critic
    6, Mercury
Crocodile
    Pluto
Crops
    4, 6, Moon
Crossing a border
    9
Crowds of people
    Moon

Astrological Keywords

Crown
    Leo
Crow
    Capricorn
Cruel
    Leo
Cruelty
    Mars, Pluto
Crutches
    Capricorn
Crying
    12, Neptune
Crystal ball
    Neptune
Crystal stone
    Moon, Saturn, Cancer
Cucumber
    Moon, Sagittarius
Cultivator
    Saturn
Cultural knowledge
    9, Jupiter
Culture
    9, Venus
Cupboard
    Moon, Virgo
Cupboard, high
    Libra
Curiosity
    Mercury
Curious
    Gemini
Currants
    Jupiter
Customs
    2, Venus
Customs fees and tariffs
    Capricorn
Customer
    7
Customs official
    Capricorn
Cut to the quick
    Scorpio
Cut
    8, Mars, Aries
Cutting
    Mars

Cyclone
    Uranus
Cyprus tree
    Saturn, Venus
Cyprus
    Taurus

# D

Daily comings and goings
   3, Mercury
Daily duties
   6
Daily life
   Moon
Dairy
   Moon
Dairy barn
   Taurus
Dairy equipment
   Taurus
Dairy farmer
   Taurus
Damage from earthquake
   4
Damage from natural disaster
   4
Damage
   8
Dancer
   Venus, Pisces, Pluto
Dance
   5
Dancing
   Venus, Neptune
Dancing teacher
   Libra
Dandelion herb
   Sun, Jupiter, Leo
Danger
   8, Mars, Pluto, Saturn
Dare, to
   Aries
Daring
   Mars
Dark corner
   Capricorn
Dark place
   Saturn, Capricorn
Date (fruit)
   Libra, Pisces
Dating
   5, Venus, Sun

Daughter-in-law
   11
Dawn
   Sun
Dawn of a new day
   Aries
Day laborer
   6
Day, new
   Aries
Daydreaming
   12, Neptune
Daylight
   Sun
Deafness
   Saturn, Capricorn
Dealer
   3, Mercury
Dealer in liquids
   Moon
Deal
   7
Dearest wish
   11
Death
   8, Mars, Saturn, Scorpio
Death and regeneration
   Pluto
Death of a parent
   5, 11
Death of a pet
   1
Death of a career
   5
Death of others
   2, Venus
Death of someone inquired about
   2, 8
Death, cause of
   8
Death, losses and gains because of
   8
Death, physical and spiritual
   8, Pluto

Death, sudden
   Uranus
Death in the family\
   11
Debts
   8, Saturn, Scorpio
Debut
   1
Decay
   8, Pluto, Saturn
Decaying matters
   Pluto
Deception
   12, Neptune
Decision of the court in a lawsuit
   4, 1
Decision
   3, Mercury
Decorations
   5
Decorative arts
   Venus
Decorator
   Venus
Deed, written
   3, Mercury
Deep
   Pisces
Deer
   Venus
Defeat
   12, Saturn, Neptune
Defect of character
   12, Neptune
Defendant in lawsuit
   7
Difference
   6, Mars
Defiance
   Uranus, Mars
Degeneration
   Pluto
Delay
   Saturn, Neptune

*Astrological Keywords*

Deliberation of a jury
   6
Delight
   5
Delirium
   Mercury
Delivery
   3, Mercury
Delivery person
   3, Mercury
Delusion
   12, Neptune, Gemini
Demise
   8, 4
Democrat
   Saturn
Democratic
   Gemini
Demonstration, street
   Aquarius
Den
   Virgo
Denim
   Saturn
Denmark
   Aries
Dental problem
   Saturn
Dentist and dentistry
   6, Mars
Department store
   10
Dependable
   Taurus
Dependent
   6, Mercury
Diplomacy
   Juno
Depression
   Saturn, Moon
Deprivation
   Saturn
Depth
   Saturn
Dermatitis
   Capricorn
Dermatologist
   Capricorn

Desert
   Aries, Capricorn
Designer
   Venus
Desirability
   Venus
Desire for action
   1
Desires
   11, Moon, Mars
Desk
   3, Mercury, Mars, Gemini
Destroyer
   8, Saturn
Destruction
   8, Pluto
Destructive
   Opposition
Detachment
   Uranus
Details and detailing
   6, Mercury, Capricorn, Virgo
Detective
   12, 8, Pluto, Scorpio
Detention
   12, Neptune
Detention center, juvenile
   12
Determined
   Taurus, Scorpio
Detour
   Uranus
Deviation from the norm
   Uranus
Devotion
   Neptune
Dexterity
   Mercury
Dexterous
   Gemini
Diabetes
   Venus, Jupiter, Libra
Diamond merchant
   Capricorn
Diamond mine
   Capricorn
Diamond miner
   Capricorn

Diamond stone
   Sun, Saturn, Aries, Leo, Capricorn
Diaphragm
   Cancer
Dairy
   3
Dice
   Pluto
Dictator
   10, Uranus, Pluto
Dictatorship
   Pluto, Scorpio
Diet
   6, Mercury, Virgo
Diet deficiency
   Virgo
Diet deficiency disease
   Virgo
Dietary habit
   6
Dietitian
   6, Mercury, Virgo
Diffusion
   Neptune
Digestion
   Moon, Virgo
Digestion, process of
   Virgo
Digestive disorder
   Virgo, Cancer
Digging up
   4, Moon
Dignified
   Leo
Dignitary
   10, Sun
Dignity
   10, Sun
Dill herb
   Mercury, Virgo
Dining out
   5
Dining room
   10, Sun, Venus
Dinner engagement
   5
Diphtheria
   Venus, Cancer, Taurus

Diploma
  9
Diplomacy
  Venus
Diplomatic
  Libra
Diplomats
  Venus, Jupiter, Sagittarius
Diplomat from foreign country
  5
Direct
  Sagittarius
Director, theatrical
  Leo
Disadvantage
  Saturn
Disagreeable duty
  6
Disappearance
  Pluto
Disappointment
  12
Disasters, natural
  4, 8
Discarded things
  Pisces
Discipleship
  6
Discipline
  Saturn
Discipline and one who enforces it
  10, Saturn, Capricorn
Disciplined thought
  9
Discriminating
  Virgo
Discrimination
  6, Mercury
Discussion
  3, Mercury
Disease
  6
Disease caused by excess
  Jupiter
Disease, fear
  Virgo
Disease, sexually transmitted
  8
Disease caused by insect
  Scorpio
Disease and the bloodstream
  Aquarius
Disease caused by emotional problems
  Cancer
Disease genetically transmitted
  Pisces
Disease of childhood
  Cancer
Disembodied entity
  8
Disheartening
  Saturn
Dishonor
  Saturn
Displaced person
  12, Neptune
Display or ostentation
  5, Sun
Disposition, natural
  1
Dispute
  7
Disruption
  Uranus
Dissemination of knowledge
  9, Mercury
Dissipation
  5
Dissipation of energy
  Saturn
Dissolution of partnership
  7
Dissolution of boundaries
  Neptune
Dissolving
  Neptune
Distance, things at a
  9
Distant connection
  9
Distant contact or interest
  9
Distant people
  9
Distant place
  9
Distant relative
  9
Distant shores
  9
Distemper
  Mars
Distress and distressing condition
  6
Disturbance, origin of
  9
Ditch
  Cancer
Diver
  Pisces
Diverticulitis
  Virgo
Divination
  9, Jupiter
Divorce
  7, Uranus
Divorce lawyer
  Libra
Divorce proceeding
  9
Dock
  Moon
Doctor to querent
  7
Doctor's office
  12, 6
Doctor
  6, Mercury
Doctor of civil law
  Jupiter
Document
  3, Mercury, Gemini
Doer
  Mars
Dog
  6, Mercury
Dolphin
  Venus
Domestic
  Taurus, Cancer
Domestic affairs
  4, Moon
Domestic chore
  6, 4

Domestic interest
    4
Domestic servant
    6
Domestic worker
    Cancer
Domesticity
    Moon
Denomination
    Pluto
Domineering
    Aries, Capricorn
Domino
    Gemini
Donation
    8
Doom
    12, Saturn
Door-to-door salesperson
    Gemini
Door
    Saturn, Capricorn
Dormitory
    4
Dove
    Venus
Dowdy
    8
Drain
    Scorpio
Drama
    Sun, Venus, Leo
Dramatic
    Leo
Dramatist
    Leo
Drastic event
    Pluto
Drawer
    6
Drawer, secret
    Scorpio
Dream and sleep patterns
    12
Dreamer
    Neptune
Dreams and visions
    9, Neptune, Pluto, Pisces

Dreams as mental journeys
    9
Dress designer
    Libra
Dressmaker
    Venus, Virgo
Drink trade
    Neptune
Driving
    3, Mercury
Driving test
    3
Dropsy
    Cancer
Drowning
    Neptune
Drudgery
    6, Mercury
Drug
    6, 12, Neptune, Pluto, Pisces
Drug addiction
    12, Neptune, Pluto, Pisces
Drug addict
    Pisces
Drug dealer
    12, Neptune, Pisces
Drugstore
    6, Virgo
Druggist
    6
Drugs, illicit
    12, Neptune
Drums
    Mars
Drunkard
    12, Neptune, Moon
Drycleaner
    6, Mercury
Dry cough
    Mercury
Dry pasture
    Aries
Dual
    Gemini
Duck
    Moon
Duel
    7, Mars

Dues
    12
Duke
    10
Dullness
    Saturn
Dump
    8, Saturn, Pluto
Dungeon
    Pisces
Duodenum
    Virgo, Pisces
Duties, daily
    6, Mercury
Duty
    Saturn
Dwelling
    4
Dwelling, temporary
    Aries
Dynamic
    Aries
Dynamic action
    Square
Dynamite
    Uranus
Dysentery
    Virgo

# E

E.S.P.
  Neptune
Eager
  Aries
Eagle
  Mars
Ear
  Taurus
Ear, left
  Mars
Ear, right
  Saturn
Earl
  10
Early home life
  4
Early morning
  Aries
Earnings
  2, Venus
Earning capacity
  2, Venus
Earth
  Saturn
Earthquake
  Uranus
Ease
  Trine
Easily deterred
  Libra
East
  1, Aries
Eastern Poland
  Taurus
Easy way out, with no growth
  South Node
Easy, taking the easy way out
  South Node
Eating habits
  6
Eating, fussy
  Virgo
Eave
  Aquarius

Ebony
  Saturn
Eccentric
  Uranus, Aquarius
Eccentric people
  11, Uranus, Aquarius
Eccentricity
  Uranus
Ecology
  4
Economic outlook
  2
Economical
  Capricorn
Economist
  Saturn
Economy
  2, Venus
Eczema
  Capricorn
Editor and editing
  3, Mercury
Education
  3, 5, 9, Mercury, Jupiter
Education, adult class
  9, Jupiter
Education, high school
  7
Education, elementary
  3
Education, higher
  9, Jupiter, Sagittarius
Education lower
  3, Mercury
Education, junior high
  5
Education, religious
  9
Education, secondary school
  Leo
Education, specialized
  12, 9
Educational advancement
  3

Educational institution, relations with
  9
Educational, matters
  5
Educational, pursuits
  5
Educator
  9, Jupiter
Effeminate
  Venus
Efficiency
  6, Mercury
Efficient routine
  6, Mercury
Effort to get ahead
  1, Mars
Efforts to promote self
  5
Egg
  Cancer, Sagittarius, Pisces
Egotism
  Sun
Egotistic
  Capricorn
Egotistical
  Uranus, Aries
Egypt, lower
  Gemini
Egypt, upper
  Libra
Ejection
  Pluto
Elderberry herb
  Venus
Elderly, the
  4, Saturn
Elder
  4, Saturn
Elected representative
  Aquarius
Election
  5, Aquarius

Electorate
  Moon
Electric
  Uranus
Electrical appliance
  Uranus
Electrical engineer
  Uranus
Electrician
  11, Uranus
Electricity
  Uranus
Electronics
  Aquarius
Elegant house
  Libra
Elementary school
  Gemini
Elephant
  12, Jupiter
Elimination
  8, Pluto
Elimination, process of
  Scorpio
Elk
  Aquarius
Eloquent
  Mercury
Email
  3, Gemini
Emancipation
  Uranus
Embargo
  Saturn
Embezzle
  Jupiter
Embezzlement
  Neptune
Embroidery
  Venus
Embryo
  Moon, Cancer
Emerald stone
  Venus, Taurus, Cancer
Eminent people
  10
Emotional
  Pisces, Cancer

Emotional attachments
  Venus
Emotional, capacity and technique
  Mercury
Emotional desires
  5, 11
Emotional expression
  5
Emotional needs
  4, Moon
Emotional problems
  12, Moon, Neptune, Cancer
Emotional security
  4, Moon
Emotionally inhibited
  Moon, Pisces
Emotions
  Moon
Emotions, feeling misunderstood
  Pisces
Emotions, intense
  8
Emotions, pleasurable
  5
Emperor
  10, Sun
Emphasis
  Conjunction and parallel
Ephemeris
  Saturn
Emphysema
  Gemini
Employee
  6, Mercury, Virgo
Employer
  10, Sun, Saturn
Employer's financial condition
  11
Employment
  6, 10, Saturn
Employment matters
  6
End of tenth house parent
  1
End of career matters
  1
End of existence
  4

End of life
  4
End of long-term affairs
  4
End of the matter
  4
Ending
  4, 12, Pluto
Endocrine gland
  Neptune
Endurance
  Saturn
Enemies in general
  12
Enemy, open
  7
Enemy, secret
  12, Uranus, Pluto, Pisces
Energy
  Sun, Mars
Engineering
  Mars
Engineer
  Mars
England
  Aries
England, political affairs
  Aquarius
England, west of
  Gemini
Engraver
  Venus
Enjoyment
  5, Venus
Entertainer
  5, Sun, Venus
Entertainment
  5, Sun, Venus
Enthusiasm
  Mars, Sagittarius
Entrepreneur
  Jupiter
Environment in general
  3
Environmental pollution
  Neptune
Envy
  Saturn

Epidemics
    8, 12, Mars, Pluto, Virgo
Epidermis, outer
    Capricorn
Epigastric region
    Cancer
Epilepsy
    Moon, Aries, Aquarius
Equality
    Libra
Equipment
    6
Equipment, electrically operated
    Uranus
Equipment, scientific
    Neptune
Equipment, stable
    Saturn
Errand
    3
Error in judgment
    12, Neptune
Escape from bondage
    12, Jupiter, Uranus
Escape from penalty
    Jupiter
Escaped convict
    7, 12
Escapism
    12, Neptune
Escrow account
    8
Escrow on property
    8
Esophagus, upper part
    Taurus
Espionage
    Pluto, Pisces
Estate administrator
    Capricorn
Estate of the father
    5
Estates (land, real estate)
    4
Estate of a deaceased person
    Capricorn
Esthetic sensibility
    Neptune

Estrangement
    12, Uranus, Neptune
Ethical responsibility
    9
Ethics
    9, Jupiter, Sagittarius
Eustachian tube
    Taurus
Evasion
    Neptune
Evening
    Moon
Everyday duty
    6, Mercury
Exacting
    Virgo
Exaggeration
    Neptune
Exaggerative
    Sagittarius
Examination
    3, 5, 9, Mercury
Examination, oral or written
    3
Excess
    5, Jupiter
Excess, getting rid of
    Scorpio
Exchange
    8
Excitement
    Uranus
Exciting place
    Uranus
Excrement
    Pluto
Excretion
    8
Executioner
    8, Scorpio
Executive
    10, Sun, Saturn, Aries, Scorpio, Capricorn
Executive acumen
    Saturn
Executive, head of an enterprise
    10
Executive work
    10, Sun

Exhaust System
    8
Exhibitionism
    5, Sun
Exotic lands
    9
Expansion
    9, Jupiter
Expansiveness
    Jupiter
Expelled party
    7
Experience
    4
Experiencing
    Cancer
Exploited, those who are
    Pisces
Exploration
    3
Explorer
    9, Aries, Sagittarius
Explosion
    Uranus
Explosive
    Mars
Export
    9
Expression
    5, Mercury
Expressive
    Gemini, Leo
Extension
    9
External sex organ
    8, Mars, Pluto
Extremes
    8, Pluto
Eye
    Aries
Eye, infection or injury
    Leo
Eye, left on female
    Sun
Eye, left on male
    Moon
Eye problem
    Sun, Aries

Eye, right of female
    Moon
Eye, right of male
    Sun
Eyebright herb
    Sun, Leo, Aries
Eyeglasses
    6

# F

F.B.I.
  Pluto
Fabric, elegant
  Libra
Fabric, transparent
  (e.g., nets and veils)
  Neptune
Façade
  1
Face
  1, Mars, Aries
Face injury
  Mars
Facing reality
  Saturn
Fact-finding
  Virgo
Factory
  4
Failure
  12, Saturn, Neptune
Faint
  Moon
Fainting
  Leo
Fair
  Sagittarius, Libra
Fairness
  Venus, Jupiter, Juno
Fair (event)
  Taurus
Faith
  9, Jupiter, Neptune
Falcon
  Libra
Fall from power
  10, Saturn
Fall
  Saturn
False appearance
  Neptune
False teeth
  6, Neptune

Fame
  10, Sun
Fame, giver of
  Sun
Family
  4, Moon, Cancer
Family affairs
  4, Moon
Famine
  8, Saturn
Famous person
  10, Sun
Fan
  Neptune
Fantasy
  Neptune
Faraway people
  9
Far neighbor
  9
Farmer
  4, 6, Saturn, Mercury
Farm
  4
Fatalistic
  Capricorn
Fate
  10, Pluto
Fateful loss
  8
Father
  4, Sun, Saturn, Capricorn
Father's kin
  6
Father-in-law
  10
Fatigue
  6, Saturn
Favorite activity
  5
Favoritism
  Lilith
Favor
  Jupiter, Venus

Fears and worries
  8, 12, Saturn
Fear of disease and poverty
  Virgo
Fear of abandonment
  Juno
Fear of ridicule
  Leo
Feces
  8
Feeling of security
  4, Moon
Feelings
  Moon, Cancer
Fees
  8
Feet
  12, Neptune, Pluto, Pisces
Foot deformity
  Pisces
Foot damage
  Pisces
Feet, veins in
  Pisces
Feldspar
  Moon
Fellow employee
  6, Mercury
Female function
  Moon
Female relations
  Venus, Moon
Female things
  Venus
Fence
  Saturn
Fennel herb
  Virgo
Fern
  Cancer
Ferryman
  Moon
Fertility
  5, Moon, Taurus, Ceres

*Astrological Keywords*

Festival
 5
Fever
 Sun, Mars, Aries, Leo
Fever, high
 Sun, Leo
Fiancé
 7
Fickle
 Gemini, Libra
Fickleness
 Moon, Mercury
Fiddle
 Neptune
Fields
 4, Taurus
Fields of grain
 Taurus, Virgo
Fierce
 Scorpio
Fighter
 Mars
Figs
 Pisces
File cabinet
 3, 6, Mercury
Files
 Mercury
Film actor
 5, Neptune
Film
 12, Neptune
Final outcome of any question
 4
Final resort
 4
Final resting place
 4
Finances
 2, Jupiter, Venus, Part of Fortune
Finances of spouse or partner
 8
Financial abundance
 Jupiter
Financial advisor
 8
Financial assistance
 2

Financial conditions of partnership
 8
Financial matters
 2, Venus, Part of Fortune
Financial obligations of the querent
 2, 8, Saturn
Financial relations with competitor
 8
Financial settlement
 2, 8
Financial speculation
 5
Financial transaction
 2
Fine art
 7, Venus, Neptune
Finery
 Venus
Fine
 8
Finger
 3, Mercury
Fire
 Mars
Firefighter
 Leo, Mars
Firearms
 Mars
Firefly
 Sun
Fireplace
 5, Sun, Mars, Leo
Fire, forest
 Sagittarius
Fish
 Neptune, Aries, Cancer, Aquarius, Pisces
Fish pond
 Pisces
Fisherman
 Moon, Neptune, Pluto, Pisces
Fixed in opinion
 Aquarius
Flatterer
 11
Flattery
 Neptune
Flatulence
 Cancer

Flea
 Pluto
Flighty
 Gemini
Flings and love affairs
 5, Venus
Flint stone
 Sagittarius, Scorpio
Flirtation
 5, Venus
Florist
 Venus
Flow
 Trine
Flower garden
 Libra
Flower
 Venus
Fluctuation
 Moon
Fluid, balance of the body
 Moon
Fluid retention
 Moon
Flying
 Uranus
Flying saucer
 9
Focus of things
 1
Fog
 Neptune, Pluto, Pisces
Follow through, lacking
 Taurus
Food
 6, Mercury, Moon, Ceres
Food industry
 6
Food, market
 6
Food preparation
 6
Food service
 6
Food stamps
 12
Food, place where food is kept
 4, 6

Food, where food is distributed
  6
Food, health
  6, Mercury
Foolhardiness
  5
Footman
  Mercury
Footstool
  Taurus
Force
  Mars, Pluto
Forecasting
  9, Jupiter
Foreign affairs
  Jupiter
Foreign associates
  9
Foreign correspondence
  Sagittarius
Foreign country
  9, Sagittarius
Foreign item
  9
Foreign policy
  Sagittarius
Foreign service
  Sagittarius
Foreign spy
  12
Foreigner
  9, Jupiter
Foreman
  10, Sun, Saturn
Forest fire
  Sagittarius
Forgiving
  Pisces
Forrester
  Leo, Libra
Forest
  Leo
Forger
  Mercury, Gemini
Forge
  Mars
Forgetfulness
  12, Neptune

Form
  Saturn
Formality
  9
Fortifications
  4
Fort
  Leo
Fortune
  Jupiter
Fortune, good
  Jupiter, Venus, Part of Fortune
Forum
  Libra
Fossil
  Saturn
Foster child
  11
Foundation
  Saturn
Foundations in general
  4
Foundation of a building
  4, Saturn
Foundling
  Pisces
Fox
  Mercury
Fragrance
  Neptune
France
  Leo
Frankfurt
  Libra
Frankincense
  Sun
Fraternal groups and organizations
  11, Aquarius
Fraud
  12, Neptune, Pluto
Fraudulent scheme, grand
  Neptune
Free thinker
  11, Uranus
Freedom
  5, 12, Sun, Uranus, Jupiter
Freedom-loving
  Uranus, Jupiter, Sagittarius

Freedom, concept of
  5, 9, Jupiter, Uranus
Freedom, gaining of
  12, Jupiter, Uranus
Friction
  Semi-square
Friday
  Venus
Friend of a friend
  9
Friendly help
  11
Friend
  3, 11
Friend's health
  4
Friend, child of
  3
Friend, close
  7
Friend, get-together with
  11
Friendship
  11, Uranus, Jupiter
Friendship, ties of
  11, Uranus
Fruit grower
  Scorpio
Fruitful
  Venus
Fruit
  Jupiter
Frustration
  12, Saturn, Neptune
Frustration that causes illness
  12, 6, Neptune, Saturn
Fugitive
  7, Moon
Fugitive, hiding place
  Aries
Fun
  5, Venus, Sun
Fun house
  5
Functional item
  Virgo
Functioning
  Moon

Funeral
    12, Saturn, Pluto, Capricorn
Furnace
    Mars, Aries
Furniture
    4, 6, Venus, Jupiter
Furniture factory
    Libra
Furniture garden
    Venus
Furniture, luxury
    Venus
Fur
    Jupiter, Leo, Capricorn
Fuse box
    Uranus
Fussing
    Virgo
Future
    2
Future-minded
    Aquarius
Future plans
    9, 11
Future, foreseeing the
    9
Futuristic
    Uranus

# G

Gadgets
  3, 11, Gemini
Gain
  North Node
Gaining publicity
  Moon
Gain by long journey
  10
Gain through science
  10
Galicia Spain
  Pisces
Gallbladder
  Pluto, Leo, Virgo
Gallery
  4
Gambler
  Sagittarius
Gambling, illicit
  12
Gambling, insolvency from
  8
Gambling, lottery and gaming wheels
  5, Jupiter, Sun, Sagittarius
Game meat
  Leo
Game preserve
  12, Jupiter
Game room
  Gemini
Game warden
  Leo
Game
  5, Sun
Game of chance
  5
Gang, street
  Scorpio
Gangster
  Pluto, Scorpio
Garage
  3, Mercury, Uranus

Garbage can
  8, Pluto
Garbage disposal
  8, Pluto
Gardener
  4, Saturn, Cancer
Garden
  4, Venus, Scorpio
Garden, flower
  Libra
Garden, roof
  Aquarius
Garlic
  Mars, Gemini
Garment bag, leather
  Capricorn
Garnet stone
  Mars, Aries
Gas
  Neptune
Gas line
  Neptune
Gases
  Neptune, Uranus
Gastroenteritis
  Virgo
Gate
  Capricorn
Gathering of facts
  3, Mercury
Gauge
  6, Mercury
Geese
  Moon
Gelatin
  Neptune
Gem
  Venus
Gender of the fetus
  5
Gender stereotype
  Lilith
Genealogy
  Saturn

General public
  7, Moon
General trade
  3, Mercury
General well-being
  1, Sun
Generalization
  9
General
  Libra
Generator
  Uranus
Generosity
  Sun, Jupiter
Generous
  Leo, Sagittarius
Gene
  Pisces
Genetically transmitted disease
  Pisces
Genital disorder
  Pluto
Genital
  8, Scorpio
Genoa
  Cancer
Genus
  Uranus
Germany
  Aries
Germs and infections, fear of
  Virgo
Gestation
  Moon
Ghetto
  12, Neptune, Scorpio, Pisces
Ghost town
  12
Ghost
  11, 12, Neptune, Uranus, Pisces, Pluto
Giddiness
  Mercury

Astrological Keywords

Gifts and legacies
: 8, Venus
Gift you give
: 2
Ginseng herb
: Mars, Scorpio
Give, must
: South Node
Give, where you must
: South Node
Giving love
: 5
Glamour
: Neptune
Gland
: Moon
Glandular secretion
: Moon
Glass
: Neptune, Sagittarius
Glaucoma
: Sun
Glee club
: Taurus
Glory
: 10, Sun
Gloves
: Venus
Glue
: Saturn Goals 11
Goat
: 6, Saturn, Capricorn
Goat shed
: Capricorn
Godchild
: 11
Going abroad
: 9
Goiter
: Taurus
Gold, items made of
: Leo
Gold metal
: Sun, Leo
Goldenrod herb
: Venus
Goldsmith
: Sun, Leo

Golfer
: Jupiter
Gonorrhea
: Scorpio
Goods on a shelf
: Venus
Gossip
: 3, Mercury, Gemini
Gossiper
: 3, Mercury
Gout
: Moon, Pluto, Sagittarius, Pisces
Governing authority
: 10, Sun, Saturn
Government
: 10, Saturn, Sun
Government agency
: 10
Government official
: 10, Sun
Government representative
: 5
Government, affairs of
: 10
Government, dealing with
: 10
Government, head of
: 10, Sun
Government, objects of importance
: Pluto
Governor
: 10, Capricorn
Grace
: Venus
Graduation
: 9
Graduation cap and gown
: Jupiter
Grain
: 6
Granary
: Taurus, Virgo
Grandchildren
: 9
Grandfather (maternal)
: 1
Grandfather (paternal)
: 7

Grandiosity
: 5, Sun
Grandmother (maternal)
: 7
Grandmother (paternal)
: 1
Grandparents
: 1, 7
Grain
: Ceres
Granite
: Saturn
Grant
: 8, Sun
Grape
: Taurus
Graphology
: Mercury
Gratification
: 5
Gratuity
: 8
Grave
: 4
Gravedigger
: 4
Gravel and sand pits
: Libra
Gravity
: Saturn
Gray
: Capricorn
Great grandchildren
: 1
Greece
: Virgo, Capricorn
Greedy
: Taurus
Grief
: 12, Neptune
Grim Reaper
: Saturn
Groceries
: Moon
Grocery store
: 6, Mercury, Virgo
Groin
: Scorpio

Grotto
  Cancer
Ground, close to
  Taurus
Ground, muddy
  Scorpio
Ground, the
  4
Group, acting as an entity
  1
Group activity
  11, Uranus
Group as a source of power
  Pluto
Group, connection
  11
Group gathering
  11
Group interest
  11
Group work
  Aquarius
Group, ties with
  11
Group, fraternal
  11
Growth
  Moon, Jupiter, Semi-sextile
Growth, slow
  Pluto
Guard
  12, Mars
Guardian
  10, Saturn, Sun
Guest room
  Venus
Guide
  Mercury
Gullible
  Neptune
Gun
  Mars
Gun shooter
  Mars, Pluto
Guru
  9, Jupiter
Gynecologist
  Cancer, Scorpio

Gypsy
  Leo

# H

Habit pattern
  Moon
Habit, personal
  6
Hair
  Capricorn
Hair transplant
  8
Hair stylist
  Libra
Hall
  Sun
Halls in house
  Gemini
Hallucination
  12, Neptune, Pluto, Uranus,
  Gemini, Pisces
Hallway
  10
Ham radio
  Uranus, Mercury
Hamburg, Germany
  Aquarius
Hammer
  Saturn
Hand wound that is crippling
  Gemini
Handicap
  12
Handicraft
  6, Venus
Handling of others' possessions
  Jupiter
Hands and arms
  3, Mercury, Gemini
Hangar
  Uranus
Hanging
  Taurus
Hangover
  12
Happenstance
  3, 11, Moon, Mercury

Happiness, idea of
  11
Hard work
  6, Saturn
Hardening
  Saturn
Hardship
  Saturn
Hard-working
  Capricorn
Hare
  6
Harmonica
  Mercury
Harmony
  Trine, Venus
Harmony through mental activity
  Venus
Harsh
  Sagittarius
Harvest
  Ceres
Hasty
  Aries
Hate
  Mars
Haughty people
  Sun
Haunted house
  Scorpio
Hawk
  Mars
Hay
  Virgo
Hazard
  5
Hazard from natural phenomenon
  9, 4
Head of an organization
  10, Sun
Head of a body
  1, Mars, Aries
Headache
  Mercury, Aries

Healer, great of others
  Chiron
Healer who may not be able to heal self
  Chiron
Healer
  6, 8, Pluto, Mercury
Healing
  6, 8, Pluto
Healing after surgery
  9
Healing crisis
  8
Healing measure of any sort
  6, Mercury
Healing power
  Pluto
Healing waters
  Cancer
Health
  1, 6, Sun, Moon
Health (problems with), sickness
  6
Health food
  6, Mercury
Health improvement program
  6
Health matters
  6
Health, overly concerned
  Virgo
Health, poor
  6, Saturn, Cancer, Virgo,
  Capricorn, Pisces
Health, poor especially in childhood
  Cancer
Health, overly concerned with
  Virgo
Hearing
  Saturn
Hearing aid
  6, Neptune

Astrological Keywords

Hearing device
- Uranus

Heart
- 5, Sun, Leo

Heart condition
- 5, Sun

Heart, as ruled by mind
- Capricorn

Heart palpitations
- Leo

Heart specialist
- Leo

Heart, malfunction of the
- Leo, Pisces

Hearth
- Leo

Heat exhaustion
- Sagittarius

Heavy artillery
- Uranus

Heavy things
- Saturn

Heidelberg
- Virgo

Height
- Jupiter

Helicopter
- Uranus

Helpful
- Cancer

Hemmed in
- 12

Hemophilia
- Pisces

Hemorrhage
- Mars

Hemorrhoid
- 8, Scorpio

Hepatic system
- Sagittarius

Hepatitis
- Pisces

Herbs
- Virgo, Ceres

Herb, delicate
- Venus

Herb, mild
- Moon

Herb, pungent
- Mars

Herb, Sweet
- Jupiter

Herder
- Saturn

Hereditary trait
- 4

Hernia
- Aries, Scorpio

Hidden defect
- 12

Hidden factors in experience
- 12

Hidden matters
- 4, 8, 12

Hidden place
- Scorpio

Hidden problem
- 12

Hidden talent
- 8

Hidden things
- 4, 12, Pluto

Hidden vice
- 12

Hides of animal
- Saturn, Capricorn

Hiding place for fugitive
- Aries

High society
- 5

High, getting
- 5

Higher studies
- 9, Jupiter

Higher-up
- 10

Hill
- Gemini

Hillside
- Libra

Hilltop
- Libra

Hindering
- 12, Saturn, Neptune

Hippie
- Uranus

Hip
- 9, Jupiter, Sagittarius

Hiring of employee
- 6, Mercury

Historian
- Moon

History
- 4, Moon, Saturn

Hoarseness
- Mercury

Hobby
- 5, Leo

Hobby, creative
- 5

Hobbyist
- Leo

Hog
- 6

Holiday (vacation)
- 5

Holland
- Cancer

Holy object
- Jupiter

Home
- 4, Moon, Cancer

Home environment
- 4, Moon

Home for the aged
- 12

Home life
- 4

Home loving
- Cancer

Home of a neighbor
- 6

Home of a sibling
- 6

Home team
- 1

Home, mobile
- 3, 4

Home, quality of
- 4

Homeless people
- 12

Homeopathic physician
- Virgo

Home where clergyperson lives
    Sagittarius
Homosexuality
    Uranus
Honesty
    Jupiter
Honey
    Sun, Venus, Jupiter, Leo, Aquarius
Honey bee
    Leo
Honeymoon
    5, Venus
Honor
    10, Pallas
Honor and code of ethics
    Jupiter
Honors
    10, Sun
Hopes and wishes
    11
Hops herb
    Mars, Aries
Hormone
    Mercury
Horse breeder
    Jupiter, Sagittarius
Horse racing
    5, Jupiter, Sagittarius
Horse stable
    Taurus
Horse trainer
    Sagittarius
Horse, fall from
    Scorpio, Sagittarius
Horseradish
    Libra
Horse
    12, Jupiter, Sagittarius
Horse pasture
    Sagittarius
Hospitalization
    12
Hospital
    12, Neptune, Pluto
Hospital, animal
    Virgo
Host of a party
    Leo
Hot tub
    Neptune, Pluto
Hotel stay at a distance
    11
Hotel
    4, Leo
Hotheaded
    Sagittarius
House
    4
House for sale
    4
House of removals
    7
House of Representatives
    11
House servant
    6, Moon, Mercury
House walls
    Gemini
House one is buying if one doesn't own one
    4
House one lives in or owns
    4
House one plans to move to
    7
House developer
    Cancer
House, driest part of the
    Mars
House, price of
    10
Household affairs
    Moon
Housekeeper
    Moon, Cancer
Housekeeper, compulsive
    Virgo
House of detention
    12
House with extensive grounds
    Sagittarius
House, abandoned
    Scorpio
House, decayed
    Scorpio
House, elegant
    Libra
House, low in the country
    Taurus
House, modern
    Aquarius
House, vandalized
    Scorpio
Housewife
    Moon
Housing
    4, Moon
How others see one
    1
Humane
    Virgo, Aquarius
Humanitarian
    Uranus
Humanitarian activities and ideals
    11, Uranus
Humor
    Moon, Jupiter
Hunch
    Neptune
Hungary
    Sagittarius
Hunter
    Mars, Aries, Leo
Hunter, big game
    Sagittarius
Hunting
    Jupiter
Hunting expedition
    Sagittarius
Hunting gear
    Leo
Hunting grounds for birds
    Libra
Hunting injury
    Sagittarius
Hunting park or grounds
    Leo, Sagittarius
Hurricane
    Uranus, Aquarius
Hurt easily
    Cancer
Husband
    Sun
Husband in a woman's chart
    Sun

Husbandry
  6, Moon
Hyacinth (stone)
  Leo, Virgo, Sagittarius, Pisces
Hydrogen
  Neptune
Hydrotherapy
  Neptune
Hygiene
  6
Hypersensitivity
  Neptune
Hypnosis
  Neptune
Hypnotist
  12, Neptune
Hypochondriac
  6, Mercury, Neptune, Cancer, Virgo
Hypodermic
  Neptune
Hyssop herb
  Jupiter
Hysterectomy
  Scorpio
Hysteria
  Uranus

I

# I

IOU
   7
Ice
   Saturn, Pluto
Idealism
   Neptune, Trine
Idealistic
   Taurus, Gemini, Leo
Ideals
   Neptune
Idea
   3, Mercury, Gemini
Idea, new
   11, Uranus
Identity
   Sun
Idleness
   Venus
Iguana
   Pluto
Illegal
   Uranus
Illegitimacy
   Uranus
Illness
   6, Mercury
Illness due to damp cold
   Pisces
Illness of a partner
   12
Illness of a pet
   11
Illness, chronic
   Saturn
Illness, incurable
   12, Neptune
Illusion
   12, Neptune
Image
   Neptune
Imagination
   Moon, Neptune
Imaginative ability
   Neptune

Immediate outcome of an event
   7
Impartial
   Aquarius
Impatient
   Sagittarius
Impersonal
   Libra, Aquarius, Vesta
Impetuous
   Aries
Import export business
   9
Importer
   Sagittarius
Importing business
   Sagittarius
Impotence
   Neptune
Impractical
   Pisces
Impractical idea
   12, Neptune
Impressionable
   Moon
Impression one makes on others
   1
Imprisonment
   12
Imprudent
   Mars
Impulsive
   Aries
In-law
   9
Inadequacies of self
   12
Inauguration
   Conjunction, 9
Incense
   Neptune
Incest
   8, Pluto, Mars
Income
   2, Venus, Part of Fortune

Income from business or career
   11
Income from others
   8
Income property
   6
Income tax return
   8
Income, ability to add to
   2
Income, effort to increase
   2
Increase
   Venus, Jupiter
Incubator
   Cancer
Indecision
   Taurus
Indecisive
   Libra, Pisces
Indemnity for damage suffered
   9
Independence
   11, Uranus
Independent
   Aries, Aquarius, Vesta
India
   Capricorn
India and its people
   Saturn
India, northern
   Libra
Indies, West
   Virgo
Indigestion
   6, Mercury
Initiative
   1
Initiator
   Aries
Individualism
   1, Uranus
Individualistic
   1, Aquarius

Indolence
    Trine, Venus
Indolent
    Pisces
Indulgence
    5, Jupiter
Industrial Revolution
    Uranus
Industrious
    Virgo
Infamy
    10, Uranus
Infant
    Cancer
Infection caused by vermin
    Scorpio
Infectious substance
    Neptune
Inferior part of the belly
    6
Inferior
    6, Moon
Infirmary
    6, 12, Mercury
Infirmity
    6
Inflammation
    Mars, Aries
Inflammatory disease
    Mars, Cancer
Influence
    Sun
Influential person
    10, Sun
Information
    3, Mercury
Informer
    12
Ingenious
    Uranus
Ingenuity
    Mercury, Uranus
Inheritance
    Scorpio, 9
Inheritance by descent
    4, Moon
Inheritance from others
    8

Inhibited
    Capricorn
Inhibiting factor
    12, Saturn
Inhibition
    12, Saturn
Initiation of project
    1
Initiative
    Mars
Injury
    8, Mars
Innkeeper
    5
Inner development
    12
Inner resources of self
    Venus
Inner self
    Sun
Innovation
    Uranus
Inoculation
    6, Mars
Inoculation, mass
    Pluto
Inquiry
    3, Mercury, Gemini
Inquisition
    Pluto
Inquisitiveness
    Mercury
Inquisitor
    Pluto
Insane asylum
    Pisces
Insanity
    Pluto
Insanity, danger of
    Saturn Insects        8
Insect, small and annoying
    Mercury
Insect, stinging
    Mars
Inside of things
    Pluto
Insomnia
    Aries

Inspiration
    9, Neptune
Inspiration
    Trine
Installment buying
    8
Instinct
    4, Moon
Institutionalization
    12
Institution
    12
Instruction
    3, Mercury
Instrument
    Mars
Instrument, delicate
    Jupiter
Instrument, percussion
    Mars
Instrument, sharp
    Mars
Instrument, wind
    Mercury
Insurance
    8, 9, Jupiter
Insurance adjuster
    9
Insurance agent
    9
Insurance broker
    Taurus, Scorpio
Insurance company
    9
Insurance for fire and damage
    9
Insurance policy
    8
Insurance settlement
    8
Insurance, compensation from
    9
Insurance, life
    8
Insurance, unemployment
    6, 8
Intangible
    Neptune

Integrity
  Sun, Saturn
Intellect
  Mercury
Intellect, intuitive
  Uranus
Intellectual
  Uranus, Gemini, Aquarius
Intellectual activity
  3
Intellectual object
  Mercury
Intellectual pursuit
  9, Jupiter, Mercury
Intelligence
  Mercury
Intense
  Scorpio
Intensification
  Conjunction, parallel
Intensity
  Pluto
Intentions
  11
Interest rate
  8
Interior decoration
  Libra
Interpretation
  Mercury
Interstate commerce
  9
Intestinal parasite
  Virgo
Intestines
  6, Mercury, Virgo
Intestines, obstruction of
  Virgo
Intolerant
  Aries, Scorpio
Intrigue
  Neptune
Introspection
  12, Pisces
Introspective
  Saturn
Institution
  9, 12, Neptune

Intuitive
  Pisces, Cancer
Invalid, chronic
  Capricorn
Invalid, contact with
  12
Invention
  Uranus
Inventive
  Gemini, Aquarius
Inventiveness
  Uranus
Inventor
  Mercury, Gemini
Investigation
  3, 12
Investigative
  Scorpio
Investigative activity
  12
Investigator
  8, 12, Pluto
Investment
  2, Venus
Investment, non-speculated
  2
Investment, sound
  1, Venus
Investor
  2
Investigation
  5
Involuntary incarceration
  12
Involuntary service ordered by law
  12
Iran, part of
  Capricorn
Ireland
  Taurus
Iron
  Mars, Aries
Ironworker
  Mars
Iron, scrap
  Scorpio
Iron, things made of
  Mars

Irritating
  Semi-square
Irritation
  Mercury
Isolation
  Pluto
Israel, state of
  Neptune
Italy
  Leo
Italy, from Naples south
  Aries
Italy, northeastern
  Gemini
Item for practical comfort
  6
Ivory
  Saturn

# J

Jackass
  Saturn
Jade stone
  Moon, Taurus, Libra
Jail
  12
Jailer
  12
Jail
  Pisces
Janitor
  Moon
Japan
  Libra
Jasper stone
  Aries, Scorpio
Jasper, pink stone
  Virgo
Jaundice
  Jupiter
Jaw, lower
  Taurus
Jaw, upper
  Aries
Jealousy
  8, Saturn, Scorpio, Juno
Jerusalem
  Virgo
Jesuit
  9, Saturn
Jet stone
  Capricorn
Jeweler
  Venus
Jewelry
  5, Venus, Sun
Jewelry as adornment or vanity
  5
Jewelry as wealth
  2, Venus
Jewelry store
  Libra
Jewelry, costume
  Mercury

Jewelry, precious
  Leo
Job opportunity
  6
Job one seeks while employed
  11
Job where one is employed
  6
Jockey
  5, Sun, Jupiter, Sagittarius
Joint activity
  7
Joint finances
  8
Joint savings
  8
Joint venture
  7, Venus
Journalist
  3, Mercury
Journey of partner
  3, Mercury, Jupiter
Journey, long
  Sagittarius
Journey
  3, 9, Moon, Mercury, Jupiter
Journey by water
  Moon, Neptune
Journey to a distant place
  9, Jupiter
Journey, short
  Gemini
Judge presiding in a court of law
  Venus
Judge's decision in a lawsuit
  10
Judge
  10, Jupiter
Judges (as a class)
  9
Judge's gavel
  Jupiter
Judge, probate
  Capricorn

Judicial
  Libra
Judo
  Scorpio
Jungle
  Leo
Juniper
  Sun
Junk
  8, Mars, Saturn, Neptune, Pluto
Junk dealer
  Pluto, Scorpio, Pisces
Junkyard
  Pluto, Scorpio, Pisces
Jurisprudence
  9, Jupiter
Juror
  4
Jury as an executive body
  10
Jury as a counseling body
  11
Jury duty
  9
Jury in a court of law
  4, Moon
Jury room
  Capricorn
Jury, deliberation of
  6
Justice
  9, Jupiter, Saturn
Justice of the peace
  10, Sun
Juvenile
  3, Mercury

# K

Karma
    12, Saturn, Pisces, South Node
Kelp
    Neptune, Pisces
Kerosene
    Neptune
Key
    Mercury, Uranus
Khaki cloth
    Mars
Kidnap
    12
Kidnapper
    12, Pluto
Kidnapping
    12, Pluto
Kidney (stone)
    8
Kidney trouble
    Cancer, Libra
Kidney
    7, Venus, Libra
Killing
    8
Killing, assassination
    12, Neptune
Kiln
    Aries
Kin
    3, Mercury
Kindred
    3
Kindred of the spouse
    9
Kinetic
    Uranus
King
    10, Sun, Leo
Kitchen
    4, Moon, Cancer
Kite
    Aquarius
Knee
    10, Saturn, Capricorn
Knickknack
    Gemini
Knives and sharp instruments
    Mars, Aries
Knowledge, quest for
    9

# L

Labor
    6, Saturn, Mercury
Labor force
    6
Labor organizer
    Aquarius
Labor strike
    6, 12, Uranus
Labor trouble
    6, 12
Labor union
    6, 12, Uranus, Aquarius
Laboratory
    8, Uranus, Cancer
Laboratory technician
    Cancer
Laborer
    6
Laboring class
    6
Lace
    Libra
Laces
    Venus
Lack
    Saturn
Lack of circulation
    Saturn
Lack of perspective
    Inconjunction
Lack follow-through
    Aries, Gemini
Lake
    Moon, Cancer
Lakes, stagnant or polluted
    Scorpio
Lamb
    Mars
Lamp
    Leo
Land
    4, Saturn, Moon
Land, price of
    10

Land developer
    10
Land, barren fields
    Capricorn
Land, bordering on water
    Cancer
Land, eroded
    Aries
Land, fertile
    Cancer
Land, fields of grain, hay, alfalfa
    Virgo
Land, freshly plowed fields
    Aquarius
Land, highest
    Sagittarius
Land, hilly and windswept
    Aquarius
Land, hunting
    Leo
Land, in danger of flooding
    Scorpio
Land, inaccessible places
    Leo
Land, likely to flood
    Pisces
Land, muddy
    Scorpio
Land, newly excavated
    Aquarius
Land, open
    Gemini
Land, open hilly
    Sagittarius
Land, overgrown
    Capricorn
Land, pasture for horses
    Sagittarius
Land, recently cleared
    Aries
Land, sandy
    Libra
Land, slum property
    Scorpio

Land, swampy
    Scorpio, Pisces
Land, unused
    Capricorn
Land, well draining
    Gemini
Land with a pond, spring, or well
    Cancer
Land, wooded hilly
    Libra
Landlord
    10, Saturn, Cancer
Land owner
    10, Saturn
Language
    3, Mercury
Language, foreign
    9
Lapis Lazuli stone
    Taurus
Large boat
    Neptune
Large financial institution
    Jupiter
Large institution
    12, Jupiter
Large public meeting
    9
Large tree
    4, Saturn
Large wooden structure
    Saturn
Large object
    Jupiter
Laryngitis
    Taurus
Larynx
    Taurus
Last illness
    4
Last will and testament
    8
Later life
    4

*Astrological Keywords*

Latrine
    Scorpio
Launching
    1
Laundress
    Moon
Laundry room
    8, Cancer
Lavender
    Neptune
Lavender herb
    Mercury, Gemini
Lavish expenditure
    Jupiter
Law enforcement
    10
Law, codes of
    Sagittarius
Law, the
    9, 10, Jupiter
Lawbreaker
    7, Uranus
Lawn
    4
Laws of society
    Saturn
Lawsuit, defendant in
    4
Lawsuit, result of
    4, 7
Lawsuit
    7
Lawyer's office
    6, Sagittarius
Lawyer
    Sagittarius
Lawyers as a class
    9, Jupiter
Lawyer of querent in a court action
    7
Lawyer, criminal
    Libra
Lawyer, divorce
    Libra
Lazy
    Venus, Cancer, Taurus
Lead
    Saturn, Capricorn

Lead, anything made of
    Capricorn
Leader
    10, Sun, Aries
Leadership
    1, 5, Sun, Mars
Leaks of water
    Neptune
Learning
    9, Mercury
Learning, advanced
    9
Learning, higher
    9
Learning, the process of
    5
Lease as agreement
    7, Mercury
Lease as document
    3, Mercury
Leather
    Saturn
Leather goods
    Saturn
Leather merchant
    Saturn
Leather worker
    Capricorn
Leather, places that sell or make
    Capricorn
Lecturer
    3, 9, 11, Mercury, Jupiter, Uranus, Gemini
Lecturing
    3, 9, Mercury
Ledger
    Virgo
Leg cramp
    Aquarius
Leg weakness
    Aquarius
Leg, calf
    Aquarius
Leg, lower
    Aquarius
Leg, upper
    Sagittarius
Legacies from others
    8

Legal action
    7, 9, Jupiter
Legal activity
    9
Legal advice
    9
Legal affairs
    9
Legal agency
    9
Legal claim
    9
Legal contract
    7, Mercury
Legal dispute
    7
Legal partnership
    Libra
Legal practice
    9
Legal procedures and transactions
    9
Legal profession
    Jupiter
Legal question
    9
Legal, make something
    9
Legalization, the process of
    9
Legalization by ceremony or ritual
    9, Jupiter
Legislation
    11
Legislative activities and bodies
    11
Legislator
    11
Leg, from knee to the ankle
    11, Aquarius
Leg, crippling
    Aquarius
Leisure
    Venus, Jupiter
Leisure activity
    5
Lemon
    Virgo, Scorpio

Lending agency
   8
Length of life
   1
Lens grinder
   Capricorn
Leprosy
   Capricorn
Lesson learned
   12
Letter
   3, Mercury, Gemini
Let go
   South Node
Lettuce
   Gemini
Leukemia
   Aquarius
Leukemia, acute
   Mars
Leukemia, chronic
   Saturn
Liability (financial)
   8, Saturn
Liability to accident
   9, Mars
Liar
   12, Jupiter, Gemini
Liberality
   Jupiter
Liberty
   Jupiter, Uranus
Liberty loving
   Gemini
Liberty, personal
   5
Libido
   8, Mars
Librarian
   3, 6, Mercury, Virgo
Library
   Virgo
Library, great
   Jupiter
Library
   3, 12, Mercury
License (documents)
   3, Mercury

Lien
   8, Gemini
Lies and rumors
   3, Mercury, Neptune, Gemini
Life force
   Sun
Life of man
   1
Life, etheric vibration of
   Aquarius
Light
   Uranus
Lightning
   Uranus
Lightning rod
   Aquarius
Lilac
   Mercury
Limiting condition
   12, Neptune, Saturn
Limits
   Saturn
Linens
   Moon, Gemini
Linens, fine household
   Venus
Linguistic ability
   3, Mercury
Linguist
   3
Link
   3
Linoleum
   Saturn
Lion
   Sun
Liquor, rare
   Sun
Liquid
   Moon, Neptune
Liquor
   Mars, Pisces
Liquor merchant
   Pisces
Lisbon
   Libra
Literary
   Gemini

Literary ability
   3, Mercury
Literary agent
   Virgo
Literary creative output
   5
Literary person
   Mercury
Literary work
   3, Mercury
Literature
   3, 9, Mercury, Jupiter
Lithuania
   Capricorn
Litter, animal
   10
Liver
   5, Jupiter, Pluto, Virgo, Pisces
Liver disease
   Jupiter, Pisces
Liver to eat
   Capricorn
Liver, lower lobes
   Virgo
Liver, upper lobes
   Cancer
Liverpool
   Virgo
Lives in the present
   Aries
Livestock company
   6
Living
   5
Living room
   7
Lizard
   Pluto
Loadstone stone
   Scorpio
Loan
   8
Lobster
   Moon, Scorpio
Local matters
   3, Mercury
Lock
   Capricorn

Astrological Keywords

Locksmith
    Capricorn
Lodge (fraternal)
    11
Lodger
    6
Logic
    Mercury
Logical
    Aquarius, Capricorn
Loins
    Libra
London
    Gemini
Loneliness
    12
Long journey
    9
Long range plan
    9, 12
Loom
    Mercury
Loose ends
    12
Loss in general
    8, Saturn
Loss of public office
    5
Loss or damage
    2
Loss or gain
    2, Venus, Part of Fortune
Loss financial
    2, Venus, Part of Fortune
Lost item in general
    2, Venus, Part of Fortune
Lost possession
    5
Lost thing
    2, Moon, Venus, Part of Fortune
Lottery
    5, Sagittarius
Lovage herb
    Sun, Taurus
Love
    Venus
Love affair
    5, Venus

Love of pleasure
    5, Venus
Love question
    5, 7
Love, how you
    2
Love, true
    Juno
Love, receiving
    11
Loved one, dealings with
    5
Lover, male
    Sun
Lovers
    5, Leo
Love, intrigue
    Libra
Lower legislative house
    11
Lower level
    Saturn
Loyal
    Taurus
Loyalties, divided
    Lilith
Luck
    5, Jupiter, Venus, Trine
Lucky break
    9, Jupiter
Luggage
    Mercury, Capricorn
Lumbago
    Libra
Lumbar vertebrae
    Libra
Lumbar vertebrae, lower
    Scorpio
Lumber yard
    Libra
Luncheon
    Moon
Lung disease
    Mercury
Lung, trouble
    Pisces
Lung
    3, Mercury, Gemini

Lust
    Pluto
Luxuries
    Venus
Luxury building
    Libra
Lying
    5, Venus, Jupiter
Lymphatic system
    Moon, Venus
Lyons, France
    Virgo

# M

Machinery
: Mars

Machinery operated by hand
: Mercury

Machinery that brings gain
: Jupiter

Machinist
: Mars

Magazine
: 3, Mercury, Gemini

Magic
: Uranus, Pluto

Magic performed by another
: 12

Magic performed by the querent
: 6

Magician
: Uranus

Magistrate
: Sun

Magistrate court
: Capricorn

Magnetic
: Uranus

Magnetism
: Moon

Magnificent structure
: Sun

Mahogany
: Mars

Maid
: 6, Moon, Mercury

Mail
: 3, Mercury

Mailing
: 3, Mercury

Mail carrier
: 3, 6, Mercury

Main bathroom
: 8, Pluto

Main sewer outlet
: Pluto

Majesty
: Sun

Make love
: 5

Malachite stone
: Aries, Scorpio

Maladjustment, in general
: 6

Maladjustments, psychological
: 12, Neptune

Malaria
: Sagittarius, Aquarius

Male gender
: Sun

Male authority
: Sun

Male sex drive
: Mars

Malice
: 8, 12

Malicious person
: 12

Malnutrition
: Virgo

Mammal of the sea
: Pisces

Managerial ability
: Sun

Management
: 10, Capricorn

Manager
: 10, Sun, Saturn, Pluto

Manager, business
: Capricorn

Manchester, England
: Cancer

Mania
: Jupiter

Manipulation of others
: 8, Pluto, Cancer

Mansions and estates, great
: 5, Sun, Jupiter, Sagittarius

Manufacturing
: Mars

Manure piles
: Saturn, Capricorn

Manuscript
: Gemini

Manuscript as written document
: 3, Mercury

Marble stone
: Gemini, Virgo

Marine
: Neptune

Mariner
: Moon

Marjoram herb
: Mercury, Gemini

Market
: Mercury

Marketing
: 6, 9, Mercury

Maroon
: Scorpio

Marriage and unions of all kinds
: 7, Venus, Libra

Marriage counselor
: Libra

Marriage of child
: 11

Marriage vows
: 9

Marriage, discord or happiness in
: 11

Marriage, end of
: 10

Marriage, proposed
: 7

Marriage, separation
: 7, Uranus

Marriage, the partner we need
: Juno

Marsh
: Neptune, Cancer, Pisces

Martial arts
: 8, Mars

Martyrdom
: 12, Neptune, Pluto, Pisces

Masculine principle
: Sun

*Astrological Keywords*

Masonry
  Saturn
Mason
    Sagittarius, Aquarius
Mass action
  Pluto
Mass marketing, people engaged in
  Aquarius
Mass media
  Uranus
Mass production
  Pluto
Mass transit
  3
Masses
  Pluto
Mass of people
  Pluto, Moon
Masseurs
  6
Master
  10
Master bedroom
  Jupiter
Masturbation
  5, 8
Mate
  7
Materialistic
  Taurus
Maternal
  Cancer
Maternal kindred
  12
Mathematical ability
  Mars
Mathematician
  Mercury, Saturn, Gemini
Matron
  Moon
Matters of the heart
  5
Mausoleum
  Scorpio
Mayor
  10, Saturn, Capricorn
Measles
  Moon

Measuring device
  6, Mercury, Gemini
Meat
  Leo
Meat, game
  Leo
Mechanical ability
  Mars
Mechanical occupation
  Mars
Mechanical things
  Mars
Mechanic
  Mars
Medal
  Jupiter
Meddlesome
  Mercury, Uranus
Media
  3, Mercury
Mediation
  7, Venus
Medicaid
  8, 12
Medical discovery
  8
Medical profession
  Jupiter
Medicine chest
  Virgo
Medicine
  6, 12, Mercury, Neptune, Virgo
Meditation
  12
Mediumistic
  Neptune
Meeting hall
  3, 11
Meeting, large gathering
  9
Meeting, small gathering
  3, Mercury
Melancholy
  Saturn, Pisces, Taurus, Virgo
Melon
  Moon
Member of a wedding
  Moon, Saturn

Membership
  11
Memory
  Moon, Mercury
Memory problem
  Mercury
Memory, good
  Cancer
Men aged 25 to 35
  Mars
Men aged 35 to 45
  Sun
Men from the past
  Saturn
Men in general
  Sun
Men's clothes
  Jupiter
Man, young
  Mars
Menses
  Moon
Menstrual disorder
  Cancer
Menstruation
  Moon
Mental activity
  3, Mercury
Mental health worker
  6, 12, Neptune
Mental illness
  12, Neptune, Gemini
Mental pursuit
  3, Mercury
Mental strain
  6, Mercury, Uranus
Mental harmony
  Biquintile
Mercenary soldier
  Scorpio
Merchandise
  Mercury
Merchandising
  Mercury
Merchant
  Mercury, Gemini
Mercury (element)
  1, Gemini

Merger
   Aquarius
Mermaid
   Neptune
Merriment
   5, Venus, Sun, Jupiter
Mesopotamia
   Virgo
Message
   3, Mercury
Messenger as personal ambassador
   5
Messenger in general
   3, 5, Mercury, Moon, Gemini
Messenger of a republic
   5
Metal worker
   Mars
Metal, tin
   Sagittarius
Metamorphosis
   Uranus, Pluto
Metaphysician
   Uranus
Metaphysics
   9
Methodical
   Saturn, Virgo
Mexico
   Capricorn
Mice
   Virgo
Microscope
   6, Uranus
Midday
   Sun
Middle-aged person
   Jupiter
Middle level
   Venus
Midwife
   Moon
Migraine
   Aries
Military
   6, Mars
Military gear
   Mars

Military service
   6
Milk delivery person
   Moon
Miller
   Moon
Milwaukee, Wisconsin
   Scorpio
Mimic
   Gemini
Mind overly preoccupied with body
   Virgo
Mind rules heart
   Capricorn
Mind, anguished
   8
Mind, development of
   9
Mind, anguished
   8
Mind, development of
   9
Mind, heart ruled by
   Capricorn
Mind, state of
   1
Mind, subconscious
   12, Moon, Pluto, Pisces
Mind, superconscious
   9, Jupiter
Mind, abstract
   9
Mind, concrete
   3, Mercury
Mind, unconscious
   4, 8, 12, Moon, Pluto
Mindedness, absent
   12, Neptune
Miner
   4
Mineral product
   4
Mine
   4, Saturn, Scorpio
Mine, hidden wealth in
   Pluto
Mining
   4

Minister (clergy)
   9, Jupiter
Mirage
   Neptune
Mirror
   Mercury
Miscarriage
   5, Uranus
Miscarriage, danger from
   Neptune
Mischief
   12
Miser
   Saturn, Capricorn
Misery
   12
Misfortune
   12, Neptune, Saturn
Misfortune, unexpected
   12, Uranus, Neptune
Misinformation
   12, Neptune
Mislaid item
   2, 4
Misrepresentation
   Neptune
Missing thing
   2, Moon, Venus
Mission, your
   Earth
Mist
   Neptune
Mistress
   Moon, Venus
Moat
   Pisces
Mob
   11, Uranus, Mercury
Model, clothing
   Libra
Modern gadget
   11, Uranus, Mercury
Molasses
   Pisces
Moment, in the
   4
Monarch
   10, Sun

Monastery
  Pisces
Monastery
  12
Monday
  Moon
Monetary partnership
  8
Money
  2, Venus, Taurus
Money belonging to querent
  Venus, Taurus
Money by marriage
  8
Money for retirement
  8
Money from career
  11
Money from renter or tenant
  7
Moneylender
  Taurus
Money of a parent
  5, 11
Money of others
  8, Mars, Pluto
Money of a business
  11
Money of the dead
  8
Money owed the querent
  2
Money querent owes another
  8
Money, inherited
  8
Money, minter of
  Sun
Money, mother's
  11
Money, paper
  Mercury
Money, parents'
  5, 11
Money, partner's and possessions
  8
Money, person from whom one
    borrows
  7

Money, place where money is kept
  2, 8
Money, recovery of lost
  4
Money, spending
  2
Money, the public's
  8
Monkey
  Gemini
Monk
  9, 12, Saturn, Pluto, Pisces
Monument
  4, Saturn
Mood
  Moon
Moonstone (stone)
  Moon, Sagittarius, Capricorn, Pisces
Moral character
  Venus
Morality
  Jupiter, Sagittarius
Morals
  9
Morgue
  8, Scorpio
Morocco
  Scorpio
Moron
  Neptune
Morphine
  Neptune
Morality
  8, Pluto, Mars, Saturn
Mortgage company
  8
Mortgage
  8, Saturn, Pluto
Moscow
  Aquarius
Mosquito
  Pluto
Moss agate stone
  Taurus, Libra
Mother hen
  Cancer
Mother
  10, Moon, Venus, Cancer

Mother, illness of
  3
Mother, journey of
  6
Motherhood
  4, Moon
Mothering, physical
  Ceres
Mothering, emotional
  Moon
Mother's kin
  12
Motion
  3, Mercury, Mars
Motion picture industry
  5
Motion picture
  Neptune, Pisces
Motivated
  Scorpio
Motive, inner
  8
Motorcycle
  3
Mountain
  Jupiter, Gemini
Mountain climber
  Jupiter, Sagittarius
Mountain climbing
  Sagittarius
Mountaintop
  Sagittarius
Mourning
  12
Mourning clothes
  Capricorn
Mouth
  Mercury
Move, proposed location
  7
Movable possession
  2, Venus
Movement or travel, routine
  3, Mercury
Mover
  Mars
Movie
  Neptune, Uranus, Pluto

Mucus discharge
  Pisces
Mucous membrane
  Moon
Murder
  Pluto
Murder victim
  7, 8
Murderer
  7
Muscle
  Mars
Muscular system
  8, Mars
Museum
  4, Venus, Leo
Museum, fine art
  Libra
Mushroom
  Libra
Music
  Venus, Neptune
Musical
  Pisces
Musical instrument
  Venus
Musical instrument, string
  Venus
Musician (entertainer)
  5, Venus, Neptune
Mustard seed
  Mars, Aries
Myrrh
  Sun
Mystery
  8, 12, Moon, Neptune, Pluto
Mystery, unsolved
  Pisces
Mysterious condition
  12, Neptune
Mysterious location
  Neptune
Mystery
  Neptune
Mysticism
  12, Neptune, Pisces
Mystic
  Neptune

Mystique
  Neptune
Myth
  Neptune

# N

Naïve
    Neptune
Nakedness
    8
Narcissism
    5, Sun
Narcotics
    12, Neptune
Narrator
    3, Mercury
Nasal bone
    Scorpio
Natural disaster
    Uranus
Natural resource
    4
Nature of the grounds one
    purchases
    4
Naval officer
    Scorpio
Naval
    7
Navigation
    Moon, Neptune
Navigator
    Neptune
Navy
    6, 9, Moon, Neptune
Necessity
    Saturn
Necessity of life
    6
Neck
    2, Venus, Taurus
Needles
    Mercury, Mars
Negotiations
    7
Negotiations, secret
    Scorpio
Neighbor
    3, Gemini

Neighbor of spouse
    9
Neighborhood
    3, Mercury
Neighborhood activity
    Mercury
Neighborhood interests
    3, Mercury
Neighborhood, decline
    Pisces
Neighboring environment
    3
Near neighborhood
    3
Neighbors, dealing with
    3
Nephew by marriage
    1
Nephew
    7, Venus
Nerve network
    Aquarius
Nerve, illness
    Gemini
Nerves
    Mercury
Nervous
    Gemini
Nervous aggravation
    6, Mercury, Uranus
Nervous breakdown
    12, Uranus, Neptune
Nervous disease
    Mercury, Gemini
Nervous system and illness
    3, Mercury, Uranus
Nervous tension
    Uranus
Nervous twitch
    Uranus
Nervousness
    Mercury, Uranus
Nest
    Cancer

Netherlands
    Cancer
Nettle herb
    Mars
Networking
    3
Neuralgia
    Aries
Neurotic
    Pisces
New age
    Uranus
New age gadget
    11, Uranus
New method
    Uranus
New place of residence
    7
New York
    Cancer
New Zealand
    Cancer
Newcomer
    1
News
    3, Mercury, Moon
News, circulation of
    Uranus
News, receiving
    3, Mercury
News, those who brings the
    3, Mercury
Newspaper
    3, Mercury, Gemini
Niece
    7, Venus
Niece by marriage
    1
Night on the town
    5
Nimble
    Gemini
Nitty-Gritty
    8, Scorpio

No Nonsense
   8
Nobility
   Sun
Nobleman
   Sun
Nomadic
   Uranus
Nomad
   Aries
Nonconformist
   11, Uranus
Non-distinction
   Moon
Non-sectarian
   Aquarius
Normal
   Venus
Normandy, France
   Pisces
North
   4, Cancer
Northeast
   Leo, Scorpio
Northwest
   Aquarius, Pisces
Norway
   Scorpio
Notary
   3, Mercury
Note
   3
Notoriety
   10, Moon
Notorious
   Uranus
Nourishment
   Moon, Cancer
Novelty
   Uranus
Noxious Fumes
   Pisces
Nuclear physicist
   Scorpio
Nudist
   Neptune
Nun
   12, Pluto, Pisces
Nursery
   Gemini
Nursery (baby)
   Moon
Nursery employee
   Cancer
Nurse
   6, Moon, Venus, Virgo
Nurse, wet
   Cancer
Nursing
   6, Moon
Nursing home
   12
Nutrition
   6, Moon, Mercury, Venus,
   Jupiter, Ceres
Nurturing
   Ceres

# O

Obesity
    Moon, Jupiter, Taurus
Objectives in general
    11
Object made of tin
    Sagittarius
Object made of brown iron and steel
    Aries
Object made of silver
    Cancer
Object of affection
    5, Venus
Object placed under something
    Taurus
Object, broken
    Aries
Object, copper
    Libra
Object, wooden
    Libra
Obligation
    Saturn
Obscure
    Neptune
Obsession
    8, Neptune, Pluto
Obstacle
    Square
Obstacle
    10, Saturn
Obstacle, removal of
    Scorpio
Obstetrics
    Moon
Obstruction
    Saturn
Obstructive
    Square
Occult
    Uranus
Occult experience
    8

Occult matter
    8, 12, Pluto
Occult society
    12
Occultism
    Pisces
Occupation
    6, 10
Occupation involving reality
    12, Neptune
Occupation, poorly paid
    Saturn
Ocean
    Neptune, Pisces
Octopus
    Scorpio
Odd shaped thing
    Uranus
Office
    Saturn
Office (status)
    10
Office holding
    Sun
Office of an agent
    6, 9
Office of the partner
    7, 10
Office or base of operations
    4
Office or employment
    10
Office where one works
    4, 6
Office worker
    Virgo
Office, gaining an
    10
Officer in authority
    10
Office on upper floor
    Aquarius
Official
    10, Sun, Saturn

Official business
    10, Saturn
Offspring, physical or mental
    5
Oil
    Neptune, Pluto, Pisces
Oil well
    Neptune
Old age
    4, Saturn
Old people and things
    Saturn
Old, the
    Capricorn
Omen
    Moon
One's attorney
    7
One's counselor
    7
One's physician
    7
Onion
    Mars
Onyx, black (stone)
    Cancer
Onyx white stone
    Capricorn
Opal
    Libra, Aquarius
Open adversary
    7
Open enemy
    7, Venus
Open warfare
    7
Opera
    5
Operation
    Mars
Opiate
    Neptune
Opinion
    Mercury

Astrological Keywords

Opponent
  7
Opportunity
  Jupiter, Sextile
Opposite party
  7
Opposition behind the scenes
  12
Opposition, underhanded or sneaky
  12
Optimism
  Jupiter
Optimistic
  Leo, Sagittarius
Oracle
  Neptune
Orange
  Sun, Virgo, Libra
Orator
  Mercury
Orchard
  4, Scorpio
Orchestra
  Venus
Order
  Saturn
Ordinary business
  Moon
Organ donor
  7
Organic chemist
  Cancer
Organization
  10
Organizational ability
  Saturn
Organization
  11, Saturn
Organization, fraternal
  Aquarius
Organized crime
  7, 12, Pluto, Scorpio
Organized crime activity
  12
Organized labor
  6
Organizational ability
  Saturn

Origin of disturbance
  9
Orkney Islands
  Capricorn
Ornament
  5, Venus, Sun
Orphanage
  Neptune, Pisces
Orphan
  12, Neptune
Orthodox observations
  9
Orthodox religion
  9
Orthodoxy
  Saturn
Orthopedic equipment
  Capricorn
Ostentatious behavior
  5, Sun
Ostentatious item
  Leo
Osteomyelitis
  Capricorn
Other party in a contest
  7
Other people in general
  7
Other places
  7
Other side in an issue
  7
Otter
  Moon
Outbuilding
  Libra
Out of the body
  10
Outcome of contentions
  7
Outcome of illness
  9
Outcome of opposition, enmity
  7
Outcome of the matter, final
  4
Outcome of the matter, immediate
  7

Outcome
  4
Outer limits
  Saturn
Outer space
  Uranus, Aquarius
Outgoing
  Leo
Outlaw
  Uranus
Outlawed person
  7
Outlook, worldly
  1
Outspoken
  Aries
Ovarian trouble
  Cancer
Ovary
  7, Moon, Venus, Libra
Oven
  Mars, Leo
Overly tired
  6
Overalls
  Saturn
Overbearing
  Leo, Scorpio
Overexposure to heat
  Sagittarius
Overseas
  9
Overseeing
  Capricorn
Oversight
  10
Overstrained
  6
Ownership
  5
Oxen
  12
Oxford
  Capricorn
Oyster
  Scorpio

# P

Painter
  Neptune
Painter (artist)
  Venus, Neptune
Painting
  Venus
Paint
  Neptune
Pakistan, West
  Libra
Palace
  5, Sun, Leo
Palate
  Venus
Palestine
  Aries
Pallbearer
  8
Palpitation
  Leo
Panama
  Capricorn
Pancreas
  Cancer, Virgo
Panda bear
  12
Pantry
  Virgo, 4
Papers
  3, Mercury
Parade float
  Jupiter
Parade
  9, 5
Paraguay
  Cancer
Paralysis
  Saturn, Uranus
Paramedic
  Mars
Paramour
  7
Paranoia
  Neptune

Pardon
  12
Parent-child relationship
  Ceres
Parents, death of
  5, 11
Parent-in-law
  4
Paris
  Virgo
Park
  Leo
Park for recreation
  5
Parks and preservations (gardens)
  4
Parliament
  11, Uranus, Aquarius
Parole
  12, Jupiter
Parrot
  Mercury
Parsley herb
  Capricorn
Party (entertainment)
  5, Venus
Partner
  7, Venus
Partner, focus on
  Juno
Partner's room
  7
Partnership finances
  8
Partnership
  7, Venus
Partnership, legal
  Libra
Party to a contract
  7
Passionate
  Scorpio
Passion
  5, Mars

Passivity
  Moon
Passport
  Capricorn
Past mistake
  12, Neptune
Past, the
  12, South Node
Pastel
  Venus
Pasture
  4
Pasture for horses
  Sagittarius
Passage, dry
  Aries
Pasture, fertile
  Taurus
Patent
  Mercury
Paternal kindred
  6
Patience
  12, Pisces, Chiron
Patient
  Cancer, Taurus, Saturn
Patriotic
  Cancer
Peace
  Libra
Peace at any price
  Libra
Peace loving
  Libra
Peach
  Venus, Virgo, Scorpio
Peacock
  Sun
Pearl
  Moon, Neptune, Cancer
Pea
  Aries, Leo, Sagittarius
Pedantic
  Virgo

Astrological Keywords

Pediatrician
: Cancer
Pelvis
: Scorpio
Penile colony
: Pisces
Penetrating
: Scorpio
Penetration
: Pluto
Penis
: Scorpio
Penitentiary
: 12
Penny Royal
: Venus
Pension
: Scorpio
Penthouse
: Aquarius
People aged 45 to 60
: Jupiter
People aged 60 to 70
: Saturn
People aged 70 to 85
: Uranus
People in power
: 10, Sun
People of high status
: Jupiter
People, common
: 4, 7, Moon
People, forcible control of
: 10, 12, Pluto
People, important
: 10, Sun
People, other
: 7, 11
People, powerful
: 10
People, races of
: Pluto
People, sensitive
: Neptune
People, serious
: Saturn
People, sleazy
: 12

People, society
: Venus
People, trades
: 6, Mercury
People, unusual
: Uranus
Peppermint herb
: Sun, Venus, Mars, Leo, Aries
Peptic ulcer
: 6, Mercury
Perceiving
: 3, Mercury
Perceptual skill
: Pallas
Perception
: 3, Mercury
Perfection, seeks
: Virgo
Perfectionist
: Capricorn
Performer
: Venus
Perfume
: Libra
Peril
: 8, Mars, Pluto, Saturn
Periodical
: 3, Mercury
Peritonitis
: Virgo
Perjury
: Mercury
Persecution
: 12
Persecutor
: 12
Perseverance
: Saturn
Persia
: Taurus
Person holding office
: 10
Person inquired about
: 7
Person of rank
: 10
Person stealing
: 7

Person, absent
: 1, 9
Person, absent, unrelated to querent
: 1, Moon
Person, great
: 10
Personal
: Scorpio
Personal appearance
: 1
Personal belongings
: 2, Venus
Personal creativity
: 5
Personal finances
: 2
Personal interests
: 1
Personal limitations
: 12, Neptune
Personal property
: 2, Venus
Personal prowess
: 1
Personal wealth
: 2, Venus
Personality
: 1, Moon
Personnel
: 6
Person with authority over querent
: 10
Person of mature age
: Mars, Saturn
Person, missing
: 7, 9, Moon
Person, older
: Saturn
Person, religious
: 9, Jupiter
Perspective, lack of
: Inconjunct
Persuasive
: Mercury, Libra
Perversity
: Uranus, Neptune
Pessimism
: Saturn, Pisces

Pestilence
    Mars, Leo
Pest
    Mercury
Petition
    5
Petroleum
    Neptune
Pet
    6, Virgo, Mercury
Pet as surrogate child
    5
Pet, peculiar
    Pluto
Petty
    Mercury, Virgo
Pewter
    Saturn
Pharmacist
    Virgo
Pharmacy
    6, 12
Pharynx
    Venus, Taurus
Phases of the tides
    Moon
Philadelphi
    Leo
Philanderers
    12, Jupiter, Neptune
Philanthropist
    Jupiter
Philosopher
    9, 12, Jupiter, Neptune, Sagittarius
Philosophic reasoning
    Jupiter
Philosophic society
    9
Philosophical
    Sagittarius
Philosophy
    9, Jupiter, Sagittarius
Phlegm
    Pisces
Phobias
    Pluto
Phone
    3, Gemini
Phone call
    3, Mercury
Photographer
    Neptune
Photograph
    Mercury
Photography
    Neptune, Pisces
Photography supplies
    Neptune
Physical
    Leo
Physical body
    1
Physical constitution
    Ceres
Physical discomfort
    6
Physical examination
    6
Physical world, where you meet the
    Earth
Physician as querent's advisor
    7
Physician to the querent
    7
Physician
    6, 7, 9, Jupiter, Pluto
Physician, homeopathic
    Virgo
Physicist
    Aquarius
Physics
    Aquarius
Pickpocket
    Gemini
Picky
    Virgo
Picnic
    5
Pilgrim
    Moon
Pilot
    9, 11, Uranus, Neptune
Pimp
    Scorpio
Pimple on the face
    Sun
Pink
    Venus
Pin
    Mercury
Pioneering
    Aries
Pioneer
    1, Mars, Aries
Pipe dream
    12, Neptune
Piracy
    Scorpio, Pisces
Pirates
    Scorpio
Pith
    Sagittarius
Pituitary gland
    Pisces
Place of removal
    7
Place of residence
    7
Place one currently occupies
    4
Place where business is conducted
    4
Place where partner spends the most time
    7
Place where querent spends the most time
    1
Place hidden or out of sight
    12
Place near human genitals
    8
Place near water or plumbing
    5
Place of amusement
    5
Place that is high up
    9
Place where people gather
    7
Place where records are stored
    6
Place secret or hidden
    Scorpio

Place unfrequented or unexplored
    Aries
Plague
    8, 12, Mars, Pluto, Leo
Plaid
    Uranus
Planner
    Aquarius
Planning ahead
    9
Planting
    Moon
Plant
    Moon, Venus
Plastering, in home
    Aries
Plastic
    Moon, Neptune
Playground
    5, Gemini
Play, for fun
    5, Venus, Sun
Player
    Venus
Play
    5
Pleasant time
    5
Pleasurable pursuit
    5, Venus
Pleasure
    5, Venus
Pleurisy
    Gemini
Plot
    Pluto
Plots and schemes
    12
Plow
    Taurus
Plumber
    Saturn, Pluto
Plumbing problem, leak
    Neptune
Plumbing supplies
    Saturn
Pneumonia
    Mercury, Gemini

Pocketbook
    2, Venus
Pocket
    6, Virgo
Poet
    Mercury, Neptune
Poetry
    Venus
Poetry, love of
    Neptune
Poisoning
    Pisces
Poison
    8, 12, Neptune, Pisces
Poland, east
    Aries, Taurus
Poland, parts of
    Aquarius
Prussia
    Aquarius
Police
    Mars
Police as authority
    10
Police station
    Capricorn
Police, as civil servant
    6
Police, secret
    Pluto
Police officer
    Capricorn
Poliomyelitis
    Cancer
Political affairs of England
    Aquarius
Political affairs, United States
    Aquarius
Political election
    5, Sun
Political orator
    Aquarius
Political party in power
    10
Political party not in power
    4
Political preferment
    10, Sun

Political propaganda
    9, Neptune
Political strategy
    Pallas
Political success
    10
Political underground
    Pluto
Politician
    Sun, Jupiter
Politics
    Sun, Jupiter
Pollution
    8, Pluto
Pomp and circumstance
    5, Sun
Popularity
    10, Sun, Moon
Porcelain
    Mercury
Porch
    Jupiter
Portugal
    Pisces
Position in society
    10, Sun, Saturn
Physician of management
    Sun
Positions of power and authority
    Sun
Positive
    Aries
Positive objective
    North Node
Possession, movable
    2, Venus
Possess
    Taurus
Possession
    2
Possessive
    Taurus
Post office
    3, Mercury
Postal system
    3, Mercury
Postal employee
    3

Posture, poor
   Virgo
Potency
   Mars
Pottery maker
   Capricorn
Pottery
   Saturn
Poultry
   Virgo
Poultry to eat
   Libra
Pouting
   Libra
Poverty
   12, Saturn
Poverty, fear of
   Virgo
POW camp
   Neptune
Power
   10, Mars, Pluto, Sun
Power of attorney
   5, 7
Power to achieve worldly success
   10
Practical
   Saturn, Taurus, Capricorn
Pragmatism
   Saturn
Prague
   Leo
Praise
   11
Practical insight
   10
Practical sense
   Capricorn
Practical talent
   10
Prayer
   9
Preacher
   9, Jupiter
Precise
   Virgo
Precision
   6, Mercury

Predicting the future
   9, Jupiter
Preferment
   10, Sun
Pregnancy and childbirth
   5, Moon, Cancer
Pregnancy, state of a woman with child
   5
Present residence
   4
Present, the
   1
Preserving
   6
President
   10
Press
   3, Mercury
Prestige
   10, Sun, Jupiter
Pretense
   Neptune
Pretentious
   Leo
Preventive medicine
   6, Mercury
Pride
   5, Sun
Prideful
   Leo
Priest
   9, Jupiter, Saturn
Prime minister
   10
Prince
   10, Leo
Principal, school
   Capricorn
Printer
   3, Mercury, Virgo
Printing
   3, Mercury, Pluto
Printing press
   Mercury
Prison
   12
Prison camp
   Pisces

Prison system
   Neptune
Prisoner, escaped
   7, 12
Prisoner
   Pisces
Prison
   12, Saturn, Neptune, Pisces
Privacy
   4, 12
Private enemy
   12
Private investigation
   12
Private matter
   12
Private parts
   8
Private problem
   12
Private scandal
   12
Private study
   3
Privy
   Scorpio
Prize fight
   7, Sun
Prize
   Jupiter
Proactive
   6
Probate
   8, 9
Probate court
   Capricorn
Probate judge
   Capricorn
Probe
   8, Mars, Pluto
Probing
   Scorpio
Problem, personal
   12, Neptune
Procrastinate
   Pisces, Sagittarius
Procreation
   5

Produce and agriculture interests
    4
Producer, theatrical
    Leo
Profession
    10
Professional ability
    Jupiter
Professional affairs
    10
Professional associate
    Uranus
Professional class
    9, Jupiter
Professional work
    Jupiter
Professional
    9, 10, Jupiter
Professor
    9
Proficiency in a science
    9
Profit from a move
    8
Profit or gain
    2, Venus, Jupiter
Profits from a corporation
    10
Profits of a business
    11
Profits of a partnership
    8
Profits of a publication
    10
Prognostication
    9
Progressive
    Aquarius
Projects of the querent
    5
Project, new
    1
Prominence
    Conjunction and parallel
Promissory note
    Mercury
Promoter
    5, Sun

Promotion
    10, Sun
Propaganda
    9, Jupiter, Neptune
Property
    Taurus
Property, non real estate
    2, Part of Fortune
Property damage
    4
Property damage from flood or earthquake
    4
Property escrow
    8
Property matter
    4
Property tax
    8
Property, dreary
    Virgo
Property, movable
    2, Venus, Part of Fortune
Property, profitable
    Virgo
Prophecy
    9, Jupiter, Neptune
Prophetic dream
    9
Prophetic vision
    9
Prophet
    9, Jupiter
Prosperity
    Jupiter
Prostate glands
    Scorpio, Pluto
Prostitute
    8, Scorpio
Prostitution
    8, Scorpio
Prostitution, organized
    12
Protection
    9, Jupiter
Protective custody
    12
Protective urge
    Moon

Protect and confine
    Capricorn
Proud
    Leo
Provider
    Cancer
Proxy
    5
Provocative
    Aries
Prudence
    Saturn
Prune
    Leo, Virgo, Scorpio
Prussia
    Aquarius
Psoriasis
    Capricorn
Psychiatric treatment
    6, 12
Psychiatrist
    6, 11, Uranus, Scorpio
Psychic ability
    12, Moon, Neptune
Psychic influence
    12
Psychic phenomena
    12, Neptune, Pisces
Psychic
    12, Neptune
Psychoanalysis
    8, Pluto, Pisces
Psychological
    Pisces
Psychological counselor
    8, 11, Pluto, Uranus
Psychological problems
    Cancer
Psychologist
    8, Jupiter, Pluto, Uranus
Psychology
    Uranus
Psychology, deep
    8, Pluto
Psychosomatic diseases
    Moon
Pubic bone
    Scorpio

Public
    7, Moon
Public attention
    10, Sun
Public convention
    9, Jupiter
Public enemy
    7, Libra
Public face
    Libra
Public Gathering
    7
Public health
    6
Public institution
    12
Public meeting hall
    Aquarius
Public office
    10, Sun
Public opinion
    9
Public recognition
    10
Public relations
    7, 9, Venus,
Public relations worker
    Aquarius
Public school system
    5
Public servant
    6
Public status
    10, Sun
Public street
    Venus
Public teacher
    9
Public works
    6, Mercury
Public, dealings with
    Moon
Publications, ephemeral
    3
Publication, non-ephemeral
    9
Publicity
    9, 10, Sun, Jupiter

Publicity director
    9, Jupiter
Publicity, personal
    3
Publisher
    9, Jupiter, Sagittarius
Publisher's office
    Sagittarius
Publishing
    9, Jupiter, Sagittarius
Pumpkin
    Moon
Pumpkin seed
    Sagittarius
Pump
    Cancer
Punishment
    12
Pupil
    3, Mercury
Purge
    Pluto
Purification
    8, 9, Pluto
Puritanism
    Saturn
Purse
    Venus, Taurus
Pus discharge
    Pisces
Pushy
    Sagittarius
Put up with
    12
Putting one's best foot forward
    Sun

# Q

Quality of land or house
   4
Quarrel
   7
Quarrelsome
   Mars
Quarry
   Saturn, Aquarius
Quartz
   Saturn
Queen
   Leo
Querent
   1
Question
   3, Mercury
Quick-witted
   Gemini
Quicksand
   Scorpio
Quicksilver
   Mercury
Quiet
   Moon, Saturn, Taurus
Quietude
   12, Neptune

# R

Rabbi
 9, Mercury
Rabbit
 6, Moon, Venus
Race horse
 Jupiter
Racetrack
 5, Jupiter, Sagittarius
Racing stable
 Sagittarius
Radiation poisoning
 Aquarius
Radical
 Aquarius
Radical idea
 Uranus
Radical
 Uranus
Radio broadcasting
 9, Uranus
Radio commentator
 Aquarius
Radio technician
 Aquarius
Radioactivity
 Uranus, Aquarius
Radio
 Uranus, Aquarius
Radio and entertainment
 5
Radio as communication
 3, Mercury
Radish
 Mars
Radium
 Uranus, Aquarius
Raffle
 5
Railroad employee
 Capricorn
Railroad
 3, Mercury, Capricorn
Rain
 4, Moon, Neptune

Raisin
 Libra, Pisces
Ranch
 Saturn
Rancher
 4
Rank
 10, Sun
Rape
 Mars, Pluto
Rapist
 Pluto
Rash
 Aries
Rashness
 Mars
Rationalization
 Mercury
Rat
 Scorpio, Pluto
Raven
 Capricorn
Reactive
 Semi-sextile
Real estate
 4, Saturn, Cancer, Capricorn
Real estate agent
 6
Real estate developers
 Cancer
Real estate transaction
 4
Real estate, caution in matters of
 Pisces
Real estate, income from
 5
Real estate, purchasing
 4
Real estate, quality of
 4
Real estate, spouses
 10
Reality
 Earth

Realization
 10
Realization of Ambition
 10
Realtor
 Saturn
Reason
 3, 9, Mercury
Reasoning ability
 3, Mercury
Rebellious
 Uranus, Aries, Aquarius
Rebel
 11, Uranus, Aries
Rebirth
 8, legal
Receive, where you
 North Node
Receiving love
 11
Receptivity
 Moon, Neptune
Reciprocal arrangement or
 agreement
 7
Recklessness
 5, Sun, Mars
Recluse
 12, Saturn, Neptune
Recognition
 10, Sun
Record keeper
 6, Mercury
Recovered wealth
 4
Recovery of a sick person
 6
Recovery of debts
 8
Recreation
 5, Venus, Sun
Recreational sex
 5, Venus

Rectum
  6, Pluto, Scorpio
Recuperation, powers of
  Sun, Pluto, Leo
Red Tape, none
  Scorpio
Reddish complexion
  Sun, Mars
Redecorating the home
  4
Reduction
  8
Redwood
  Mars
Reeds, where they grow
  Cancer
Referee in a contest
  10
Refined
  Libra
Reflex
  Moon, Mercury
Reforms
  8, Uranus
Refrigerate
  Saturn
Refugee
  9
Refuse
  8, Pluto
Regalia
  Sun
Regeneration
  8, Pluto
Regimentation
  6
Regrets
  6
Regulation
  11
Reincarnation
  Pluto
Rejection
  Lilith
Rejuvenation
  8, Pluto
Regulations with the family
  4

Relating, deeper level
  Vesta
Relations with parents
  4
Relations with the public
  7, Moon
Relations with those in authority
  10
Relationship, platonic
  11
Relationship
  Juno
Relationship, break in
  Uranus
Relationship, clandestine
  12
Relationship, committed
  7, Venus
Relationship, contractual
  7, Venus
Relationship, equal
  1
Relationship, family
  Ceres
Relationship, foster
  11
Relationship, happy
  Venus
Relationship, hidden
  12, Neptune
Relationship, interpersonal
  7, Venus
Relationship, protracted
  Saturn
Relationship, unbonded
  11
Relationship, unequal
  6
Relative
  3, Mercury
Relative, near
  3, Mercury
Relaxation
  5
Release
  South Node
Relief work
  12

Religion
  9, Sagittarius
Religious
  Jupiter, Sagittarius
Religious affairs
  9
Religious artifact
  Sagittarius
Religious education
  9
Religious preferment
  9
Religious worker
  9
Remodeling
  4
Remorse
  Saturn
Remote place
  9, 12
Renal system
  Libra
Renewal
  8, Pluto
Renew or restored thing
  Pluto
Renovations
  8, Pluto
Rent from a tenant
  7
Rental you reside in
  4
Renter
  6
Renunciation
  12, Neptune
Reorganization
  8, Uranus, Aquarius
Reorganization
  Inconjunct
Reorganization of corporation
  Aquarius
Repair work
  6
Repellent
  Uranus
Repercussion
  Septile

Replacement for something else
  Neptune
Reporter
  3, Mercury, Gemini
Report
  Mercury
Representation of self
  5, Sun
Repression
  12
Reprieve
  12, Jupiter
Reproductive organ
  Scorpio
Reptile, armor
  Pluto
Republican
  Jupiter
Reputation
  10, Sun
Research
  8, 12, Pluto, Neptune, Gemini
Research project
  12
Research scientist
  Scorpio
Researcher
  8, Pluto
Researching new methods
  8
Reserve
  Saturn
Resident
  4, Moon
Resident while abroad
  11
Respect
  Pallas
Resort area
  5
Resort
  5, Sun
Resourceful
  Scorpio
Resourceful personnel
  2, Venus, Part of Fortune
Respiration
  3, Mercury, Gemini

Respiration system
  Mercury
Respond, how you
  2
Respond
  Taurus
Response
  1, 7, Moon
Responsible
  7, Libra
Responsibility
  10, Saturn
Possible
  Capricorn
Responsive
  Libra
Responsiveness
  Moon
Restaurant
  4, 6, Moon, Venus, Cancer, Virgo
Restless
  Aries, Gemini
Restraint
  12, Saturn, Neptune
Restricting conditions
  12, Saturn
Restructuring a corporation
  8
Result of a lawsuit
  4
Retentive
  Cancer
Retirement
  Saturn
Retirement funds
  8, 9
Retirement income
  8
Retirement, place of
  Pisces
Retreat
  12, Saturn, Neptune
Revision
  8
Revolution
  Uranus, Aquarius
Revolutionary
  Aquarius

Reward
  Jupiter
Rheumatism
  Saturn, Scorpio, Capricorn
Rhubarb
  Mars, Aries
Rib
  Leo
Ribs, upper
  Gemini
Riches
  2, Jupiter
Rickets
  Capricorn
Riding school
  Sagittarius
Rights
  2, Venus
Rights, defense of personal
  Juno
Ring
  Venus
Ringworm
  Aries
Riots
  Aquarius
Risk
  Aquarius
Rituals
  9
Revival
  7, Mars
River
  Cancer, Pisces
Road builder
  Taurus
Rival
  7, Mars
River
  Cancer, Pisces
Road builder
  Taurus
Road
  3, Mercury
Robber
  7, Marsr
Rock concert
  5

Rocket
    Uranus
Rock
    Saturn
Rodent
    8, Saturn
Roller skate
    Mercury
Romance
    5, Venus, Sun
Romance with commitment
    7
Romance without commitment
    5
Romance, idealistic
    Moon
Romantic
    Leo
Roof
    Aries, Aquarius
Rooming house
    Virgo
Room inside another
    Libra
Room, damp
    Scorpio
Roots
    4
Rope
    Saturn, Capricorn
Rosary
    Jupiter
Rosemary herb
    Sun, Leo
Roulette
    5
Royalties
    2, Venus
Royalty and nobility
    Sun
Rubber
    Jupiter
Rubbish
    8, Pluto
Ruby stone
    Mars, Leo
Rude
    Aries

Ruins
    Saturn, Scorpio
Ruler
    Sun
Rumors and lies
    3, Mercury, Neptune, Gemini
Runaway
    7, Moon
Rupture
    Uranus, Aries, Scorpio
Russia
    Uranus, Aquarius
Russia, southern
    Taurus
Russia, Georgia
    Cancer

# S

Sacral region
    Sagittarius
Sacrifice
    12, Neptune
Sacrificing
    Pisces
Saddle
    Capricorn
Sadness
    12, 8
Safari
    Sagittarius
Safe deposit box
    2, Venus, Taurus
Safe
    2, Venus, Taurus
Safety
    4
Saffron herb
    Sun, Leo
Sage herb
    Jupiter, Taurus
Sail maker
    Capricorn
Sailing
    Moon, Capricorn
Sailor
    Moon, Cancer, Scorpio, Pisces, Neptune
Sail
    Capricorn
Saint
    Neptune
Salary
    2, 11
Sales
    Mercury
Sales promotion
    3
Salesmanship
    Jupiter
Salesperson
    3, Mercury
Salesperson, door to door
    Gemini
Salon
    Libra
Salt
    Saturn, Neptune
Salvage
    6, 8, Pluto
Salvaging
    6
Sanitation
    6, 8
Sapphire stone
    Aquarius
Sarcastic
    Scorpio
Satellite
    9
Satirist
    Sagittarius
Satisfaction
    Venus
Satisfying others
    Venus
Saturday
    Saturn
Savings
    2, 8, Venus
Sawmill
    Libra
Saxifrage herb
    Moon, Cancer
Saxony
    Capricorn
Scald
    Mars
Scarlet fever
    Aries
Scar
    Mars
Scatterbrained
    Gemini
Scavengers
    Pisces
Schemes and schemers
    Neptune
Scheming
    Neptune, Gemini
Scholarly
    Sagittarius
Scholar
    3, 9, Mercury, Jupiter
School function
    5
School principal
    Capricorn
School, elementary
    3, Mercury, Gemini
Schooling
    3, Mercury
Schoolmate
    3, Mercury
School, riding
    Sagittarius
School, secondary
    5, 7, Leo
Sciatic nerve
    Jupiter, Sagittarius
Sciatica
    Moon, Scorpio, Sagittarius
Science
    9, Uranus, Gemini
Science fiction
    Uranus
Science of astrology
    9, Aquarius
Scientific
    Virgo, Scorpio, Aquarius
Scientific law
    Saturn
Scientific research
    Scorpio
Scientific society
    9
Scientist
    9, 11, Uranus, Gemini
Scientist, research
    Scorpio

Scoliosis
    Cancer
Scotland
    Cancer
Scrap iron
    Scorpio
Scurry
    Capricorn, Scorpio
Sea
    12, Cancer, Neptune, Pisces
Seafaring
    Neptune
Sea voyage
    9
Sea, product of the
    Moon
Séance room
    8
Séance
    8, 12, Neptune
Searching
    Gemini
Seashore
    Moon, Pisces
Seaweed
    Capricorn
Secluded place
    12
Seclusion
    12, Neptune
Secret agent
    Pisces
Secret agreement to defraud the public
    Pluto
Secret dealings
    8, 12
Secret enemy
    12, Pisces
Secret and enmity
    12
Secret fears
    12, Neptune
Secret organization
    12
Secret place
    Scorpio
Secret police
    Pluto

Secret Service
    12
Secret society
    12
Secret sorrow
    12, Neptune
Secretary
    6, Mercury, Virgo
Secretive
    Scorpio
Secret
    8, 12, Neptune, Pluto
Secret of sibling
    2
Securities
    2, Venus
Securities, negotiable
    2, Venus
Security
    2, 4, Moon, Cancer
Sedative
    Saturn, Uranus
Seduce
    Neptune
Seed essence
    9, Sagittarius
Seeds
    Pluto
Seeing
    Mercury
Seeing, not clearly
    Neptune
Seeking of admiration
    5, Sun
Selenite stone
    Cancer
Self
    1
Self-destruction
    12, Neptune
Self-injury
    12
Self-pity
    Neptune
Self-analysis
    12, Neptune, Virgo
Self-assertion
    1, Mars

Self-assured
    Leo
Self-centered
    Virgo
Self-centeredness
    5, Sun
Self-confidence
    1, Sun, Mars, Jupiter
Self-deception
    Neptune
Self-expression
    5, Sun, Sextile
Self-indulgent
    Taurus, Sagittarius
Self-sacrifice
    12, Neptune
Self-sacrificing
    Pisces
Self wastage
    5, 12, Sun, Neptune
Self-worth
    2
Self-hood
    1, Mars
Selfish
    Cancer
Selfishness
    Saturn
Selfless giving
    12, Neptune
Selfless service
    12, Neptune
Seller
    7
Selling
    3
Seminary
    Sagittarius
Senate
    11
Senator
    11, Jupiter
Sense of importance
    Sun, Leo
Sense of lack
    Saturn
Sensitive
    Cancer

Sensitivity
  Cancer
Sensual
  Mars, Aries, Taurus
Sensuality (not sex)
  Venus
Sentimentality
  Venus
Separation
  Opposition
Separation
  7, Uranus
Septic tank
  8, Pluto, Neptune
Serious
  Saturn, Capricorn
Seriousness
  Saturn
Servant
  6, Moon, Mercury
Servant of the country
  6
Servants quarters
  Virgo
Serve, capacity to
  6
Service
  6
Service freely given
  12
Service rendered or received
  6, Mercury
Service repair person
  6
Service to others
  6
Service, being of
  6, Mercury
Service, necessary
  6
Service, people who give
  6, Mercury
Service, volunteer
  6, Mercury
Service of repair person
  6
Serving
  6

Serving mankind
  12, Neptune
Serving others
  Virgo
Servitude
  6
Settlement of dispute
  7
Settlement, financial
  8
Sewer
  8, Pluto, Scorpio
Sewing
  6
Sewing Machine
  Mercury
Sex
  5, 8, Mars, Pluto, Venus,
  Scorpio
Sex, deeply transformative
  Pallas
Sex, more mental or spiritual than
  physical
  Vesta
Sex, orgasmic
  8
Sex object
  5
Sex organ
  8, Mars, Pluto, Scorpio
Sex, recreational
  5, Venus
Sex, use of dominance
  Lilith
Sexual
  Scorpio
Sexual Activity
  5, 8
Sexual caring of partner
  Pallas
Sexual disease
  8, Pluto, Mars
Sexual energy
  8, Mars
Sexual intercourse
  5, 8
Sexual merging
  8, Pluto

Sexual nature
  Mars
Sexual perversion
  Neptune, Uranus
Sexual pleasure
  5
Sexual power
  8, Mars, Pluto
Sexual release
  8, Pluto
Sexuality
  8, Mars, Pluto
Shame
  12
Shared asset
  8
Shared expenses
  8
Sharing
  7
Shark
  Scorpio
Sheep
  6, Mars, Aries
Sheep farmer
  Mars, Aries
Shelf for food
  Virgo
Shepherd
  6, Mars, Aries
Sheriff
  Mars
Shin
  Aquarius
Ship at sea
  1
Ship's hold
  Cancer
Shipping
  Neptune
Shipping business
  Jupiter
Ship
  Neptune
Shock
  Uranus
Shoe store or factory
  Capricorn

Shoes
   Saturn
Shop clerk
   Virgo
Shop of the querent
   10
Shopkeeper
   Moon
Shopper
   7
Shop
   6
Shoulder
   3, Gemini
Shovel
   Saturn
Shrewdness
   8, Pluto, Saturn
Shrimp
   Scorpio
Shrine
   9
Shy
   Cancer, Aquarius
Shyness
   Moon
Sibling
   3, Mercury
Sibling, dealings with
   3
Sicily
   Leo
Sick room
   6, 12
Sickle cell anemia
   Pisces
Sickness, its quality and cause
   6
Side, wound to
   Leo, 6
Sight, sense of
   Mercury
Significance
   Sun
Significant visions
   9
Sign a contract
   3
Sign papers
   3, Mercury
Sign that is read
   Mercury
Silk
   Venus
Silo
   Virgo
Silver, metal
   Moon, Cancer
Silver, object made of
   Cancer
Singer
   2, Venus, Taurus
Sink
   Scorpio
Sins of omission and commission
   12, Neptune
Sister
   3, Mercury
Skeleton
   Saturn, Capricorn
Skeleton in the closet
   12, Neptune
Skeptical
   Virgo
Skin
   Saturn, Libra, Capricorn
Skin condition
   6, Mercury, Saturn, Venus, Capricorn
Skin, sensitive
   Aquarius
Sky, things in the
   9
Skylight
   Sun
Skyscraper
   Sagittarius
Slate stone
   Capricorn, Aquarius
Slaughterhouse
   Mars, Scorpio
Slave quarters
   Pisces
Slavery
   12, Neptune
Slave
   6, 12, Neptune, Pisces
Sled
   Mercury
Sleep
   12, Neptune, Pisces
Sleepwalking
   Neptune
Sloppy
   Venus, Virgo
Slow moving
   Taurus
Slow down
   Saturn
Slowness
   Saturn
Slum property
   Scorpio
Slum
   Capricorn, Pisces
Small boat
   Moon
Smallpox
   Aries
Smith
   Mars
Smoke
   Neptune
Smother, things that
   Saturn
Snake bite
   Scorpio, Sagittarius
Snake
   Saturn, Pluto
Sneak
   12
Sociable
   Libra
Social affair
   5, 11, Venus
Social alliance
   11, Uranus
Social change
   Pluto
Social contact
   11, Uranus, Venus
Social experiment
   Aquarius
Social function
   5

Social graces
   Venus
Social Life
   11, Venus
Social place or standing
   10
Social recognition
   10
Social Security
   8, 9
Social Security programs
   6
Social skill
   Venus
Social theory
   Aquarius
Social ties
   11
Social urges
   Venus
Social workers
   Scorpio
Societies
   11, Uranus
Sociologists
   Aquarius
Sociology
   Aquarius
Softly curved objects
   Venus
Solar plexus
   6, Mercury, Virgo, Cancer
Soldiers
   Mars, Aries
Soldier, mercenary
   Scorpio
Solidification
   Saturn
Solitary pursuits
   12
Solitude
   12, Saturn, Neptune
Somnambulism
   Neptune
Son-in-law
   11
Sorcerer
   Neptune

Sorrel
   3
Sorrel herb
   Venue, Taurus
Sorrow, public
   5
Sorrows
   12, Saturn, Neptune
Sorrows, secret
   12
Sorry for Self
   Neptune, Cancer
Sot
   Moon
Soul
   5
Soul's destiny
   North Node
Sound judgment
   Jupiter
South
   10, Capricorn
South Carolina
   Libra
Southern Russia
   Taurus
Space research
   Aquarius
Spaceship
   Uranus
Spain
   Sagittarius
Spark of Life
   1, Sun, Mars
Spark
   Uranus
Spa
   Cancer
Spasmodic
   Uranus
Speaker
   3, Mercury
Speaking
   3, Mercury
Spearmint herb
   Venus, Taurus
Spectacles as sights
   Sun

Speculation
   5, Sun, Jupiter, Leo
Speculative stocks and bonds
   5
Speculator
   Leo
Speech
   3, Mercury, Gemini
Speech, slow
   Taurus
Spermatozoa and ova
   Pluto
Spices, strong (like pepper)
   Aries
Spider
   Saturn, Virgo
Spy
   12, Neptune, Pluto
Spinach
   Saturn, Cancer, Leo, Sagittarius, Aquarius
Spinal cord
   Leo
Spinal meningitis
   Leo
Spinal trouble
   Saturn, Libra
Spine
   Sun, Leo
Spine, curvature of
   Capricorn
Spinster
   Virgo
Spirit
   9, Sun
Spiritual growth
   North Node
Spiritual matters in
   12, Neptune
Spiritual progress
   Neptune
Spiritual rebirth
   8, Pluto
Spirituality
   9, Neptune, Sagittarius
Spleen
   Sun, Saturn, Virgo
Sponsor
   7

Spontaneity
    Mars, Uranus
Spontaneous
    Aries
Sporting event
    5, Sun
Sports
    5, 9, Mars, Sun, Jupiter, Leo
Sports arena
    Mars
Sports participant
    Jupiter
Spouse
    7, Venus
Spouse's health
    12
Spouse's sibling
    9
Springs
    Cancer
Stable
    Taurus
Starter
    Aries
Steel worker
    Mars
Stenographer
    3, 6, Mercury
Stepchild
    11
Steward
    6
Stir things up
    Mars
Stockbroker
    Leo
Stock exchange
    5, 11, Venus, Leo
Stock market
    5
Stockade
    Pisces
Stockholder
    5, Saturn
Stolen thing
    2, 7, Moon, Venus, Part of Fortune
Stomach
    4, 5, Moon, Cancer

Stomach cancer
    Cancer
Stomach ulcer
    Cancer, Scorpio
Stomach problem
    Cancer
Stone
    Saturn, Capricorn
Stone mason
    Capricorn
Stone quarry
    Capricorn
Stored product
    6
Storehouse
    6
Storehouse for dairy products
    6
Storm
    Uranus
Storm (incoming) in process of formation
    9
Storm, effects of
    3
Storm, violent
    Uranus
Stove
    Leo
Straightforward
    Sagittarius
Strain
    Inconjunct
Stranger
    7, 9, Jupiter
Strangulation
    Saturn, Taurus
Strategist
    Libra
Strategy
    Neptune, Libra
Street
    3, 7, Mercury
Strength
    Mars
Stress
    6
Stricture
    Saturn

Strife
    Mars
Strike, labor
    6, 12, Uranus
Strike, inception of
    6
String
    Capricorn
Strip bare
    8
Structure
    10, Saturn
Stubborn
    Taurus, Capricorn
Student
    3, Mercury
Students at a university
    Jupiter
Studies
    3, Mercury
Studio
    6
Studious
    Virgo
Study
    Mercury, Virgo, Gemini
Study hall
    Virgo
Study, love of
    Mercury
Stylish clothing
    Venus
Suave
    Libra
Submarine
    Neptune
Submerging
    Neptune
Submission
    6
Subordinate role
    6, Mercury
Subordinate
    6
Subpoena
    9
Subservience
    6

Substance
  2, Venus
Substitute
  Neptune
Suburb
  Gemini
Subversion
  12, Neptune
Success
  10, Sun, Jupiter
Success in law, science, religion
  9
Success in politics
  10
Successful venture
  Jupiter
Sudden act of God
  Uranus
Sudden break
  Uranus
Sudden or unexpected event
  Uranus
Suffering, relief of others
  Chiron
Suffering, silent
  12
Suffocation
  Neptune, Saturn
Sugar
  Venus
Suicide
  12, Neptune, Pluto, Pisces
Sunday
  Sun
Sunflower herb
  Sun, Taurus
Sunstroke
  Sun, Sagittarius
Superior
  10, Sun, Saturn
Superior, contact with
  10
Superiority
  Sun
Superstition
  4, Moon
Supplies for consumption
  2

Supreme Court
  9
Surface
  1
Surgeon
  8, Mars, Aries, Scorpio, Pluto
Surgeon, bone
  Capricorn
Surgery
  8, Mars, Pisces, Pluto
Surgery, healing after or in the future
  9
Surgical supplies
  6, Mercury
Surrender
  Neptune
Surveying equipment
  Mercury
Survival
  Sun
Suspicion
  8, Pluto
Suspicious
  Saturn, Scorpio
Swamp
  Pisces
Sweden
  Aquarius
Sweden, Lower
  Aquarius
Sweet, Addiction
  Libra
Sweethearts
  5, 7, Venus
Sweets
  Venus
Sweets, over-consumption of
  Cancer
Swim
  Neptune
Swimming
  Moon
Swimming pool
  4, Moon, Neptune
Swindler
  Neptune
Swine
  Scorpio

Switzerland
  Virgo
Sword
  Mars
Sympathetic
  Cancer, Pisces
Sympathy
  12, Neptune
Synod
  Jupiter
Syphilis
  Scorpio
Syria
  Aries
Systematic thinking
  9, Jupiter

# T

Tailor
  6, Virgo
Take background for granted
  3
Taken matters for granted
  3, Mercury
Take object in daily life for granted
  3
Take a chance
  5, Sun
Take easy way out
  South Node
Talent
  Quintile, 2, Venus
Talk
  3, Mercury
Talkative
  Gemini, Sagittarius, Mercury, Pisces
Talking
  3, Mercury
Tangerine
  Cancer
Tangible asset
  2, Venus
Tannery
  Capricorn
Tape recorder
  3, Mercury
Tapeworm
  Virgo
Tariff
  8, Capricorn
Tarragon herb
  Moon, Cancer
Task involving danger or adventure
  Mars
Taste
  Mars
Taste, good
  Venus
Tavern
  5, Moon

Tax audit
  8
Tax collector
  8
Tax consultant
  8
Tax evasion
  Pluto
Tax, income return
  8
Taxes
  8, Scorpio
Tea
  Neptune
Teacher
  3, 5, 9, Mercury, Gemini, Leo
Teaching
  5, 9
Teammate
  7. Venus
Tear duct
  Moon
Technical
  Uranus
Technician
  6, Uranus
Teenager
  Mercury
Teeth
  Saturn, Capricorn, Aquarius
Teeth, upper
  Aries
Telegram
  Mercury
Telegraph
  3, Mercury, Aquarius
Telepathy
  Uranus
Telephone
  3, Mercury, Uranus, Gemini
Telephone call
  Uranus
Telephone system
  3, Mercury, Uranus

Telescope
  Uranus
Television
  Neptune, Uranus
Temper, quick
  Mars, Aries
Temperament
  1
Temperamental
  Scorpio, Aquarius
Temporary plans
  Moon
Tenacious
  Cancer
Tenants and lodgers
  6, Mercury, Virgo
Tenderness
  Venus
Tenement
  4
Tennis
  Mercury
Tennis court
  Gemini
Tension
  square
Tent
  Aries
Termite
  Pluto
Terrorist
  12, Pluto
Tester
  Saturn
Testicle
  Scorpio
Tests and tribulations
  Saturn
Tests, written or oral
  3, Mercury
Textile worker
  Virgo
Theater
  5, Sun, Leo

Theater, owner of
    Leo
Theatrical
    Leo
Theatrical costume
    Leo
Theatrical producer or director
    Leo
Theft
    7
Theologian
    Jupiter
Theoretical research
    9
Theory
    Mercury, Saturn
Therapeutic activity
    6, 8, Mercury
Thermodynamics
    Aquarius
Thermometer
    Gemini
Thermostat
    6, Mercury, Gemini
Thief
    7, Mercury, Gemini
Thief, hiding place of
    4
Thigh
    9, Jupiter, Sagittarius
Thin, clear object
    Mercury
Thing that is noticed
    Sun
Thing that engulfs
    Neptune
Thing with sharp angles
    Mars
Thing you begin
    1
Thinking, progressive
    Gemini, Uranus
Thoracic duct
    Cancer
Thorough
    Taurus
Those dealing with future trends
    9
Those in artistic careers
    9
Those in authority
    10, Sun
Those in a ceremony
    9
Those in a confidential position
    Jupiter
Those in the film industry
    Neptune
Those in a responsible position
    10, Saturn
Those in the armed forces
    Mars
Those met in public
    7
Those of a different background
    9
Those of a different race
    9
Those of wealth and influence
    9, Jupiter
Those on welfare
    12
Those publicly noticed
    10, Sun
Those residing in querent's house
    4
Those under detention
    12
Those who cater to the pursuit of pleasure
    Venus
Those who deal with clothing
    6
Those who reside in your home
    4
Those who tend to the sick
    12, 6
Those who work beneath the surface
    Pluto
Those who work with liquids
    Moon, Neptune
Those you consult
    7
Thoughtful
    Virgo
Thoughts
    3, Mercury, Gemini
Threshold
    Capricorn
Thrill of the ride
    4
Throat
    2, Venus, Taurus
Throat specialist
    Taurus
Throat, sore
    Taurus
Throat, accidents or wound
    Taurus
Thrust
    Mars
Truth
    9
Truthful
    Sagittarius
Thursday
    Jupiter
Thyme herb
    Venus, Libra
Thymus gland
    Gemini
Thyroid
    Taurus
Tibet
    Libra, Aquarius
Tickets
    Mercury
Tics, uncontrollable
    Gemini
Tidal basin
    Pisces
Tide
    Moon
Tides of consanguinity
    3
Tiger
    Mars
Tiger Eye stone
    Leo
Tillage of the earth
    4
Timber land, cut
    Capricorn

Time
  Saturn
Time to be alone
  12, Neptune
Time, productive use of
  Saturn
Timid
  Pisces
Timing
  Saturn
Tin
  Jupiter, Sagittarius
Tips
  8
Title search
  8
Title to property
  8
Title, person's
  Sun
Title to clouded property
  Pisces
Tobacco
  Neptune
Tobacco barn
  Gemini, Libra
Toe
  Pisces
Toe deformity
  Pisces
Toilet
  Scorpio
Toledo, Spain
  Sagittarius
Tolerant
  Aquarius
Tomato
  Aries, Capricorn
Tomb
  4, Scorpio
Tongue
  3, Mercury
Tongue disease
  Mercury
Tonsillitis
  Venus, Taurus
Tonsil
  Venus, Taurus

Tool shed
  Gemini
Tool
  6, Mars
Toothache
  Saturn, Aries
Topaz stone
  Gemini, Virgo, Scorpio,
  Sagittarius, Pisces
Torment
  12
Tornado
  Uranus
Touchy
  Cancer
Tourist
  3, Mercury
Towel
  6
Town council
  11
Town square
  Libra
Town
  4
Toxic waste
  8, Pluto
Toxic waste, deposit of
  Saturn
Toy
  Leo
Tractor
  Uranus
Trade
  2, Mercury, Jupiter
Trade union
  6, 12
Trader
  Gemini
Tradesperson
  3
Tradition
  Saturn
Tradition breaker
  Uranus
Traditional
  Cancer, Capricorn
Traffic
  3, Mercury

Tragedy
  12, Uranus, Saturn
Train
  3, Mercury, Jupiter
Tramp
  Saturn
Trance
  Neptune
Transformation
  8, Pluto
Transit
  3, Mercury
Transition
  8
Transmission
  Mercury
Transmutation
  Pluto
Transport
  3, Mercury
Transport worker
  Mercury
Transportation
  3, Mercury
Transportation over long distance
  9
Transportation, means of
  Mercury
Trapper of large animal
  Leo
Trash heap
  Pisces
Travel
  3, Mercury, Uranus, Moon
Travel agent
  3, 9, Mercury, Virgo
Travel by air
  9, Uranus
Travel plans
  3, 9, Moon, Mercury, Jupiter
Travel, distant
  9, Jupiter
Travel, nearby
  3, Mercury, Moon
Traveler
  3, 9, Moon
Traveler, world
  9, Jupiter, Sagittarius

Travel of child
 1
Treason
 12, Neptune
Treasure, buried or hidden
 4, Pluto, Scorpio
Treasurer
 Leo
Treasury
 11
Treaty
 7, Venus, Libra
Treatment, medical
 6
Tree
 Venus
Tree, Bonsai or dwarfed
 Neptune
Tree orchard
 Jupiter
Tree, rare
 Sun
Tree, shade
 Jupiter
Tremor
 Gemini
Tremor, uncontrollable
 Gemini
Trial lawyer
 Jupiter
Trial
 7
Tribulation
 12
Trifle
 Mercury
Trip
 3, 9, Mercury, Moon, Jupiter
Trip, long distance
 9, Jupiter, Sagittarius
Trip, nearby
 3, Mercury, Gemini
Trip, short of partner
 9
Trivial matter
 Moon
Trotting
 3

Trousseau
 Venus
Trucker
 Capricorn
Trucks
 Sagittarius
Trudging
 3
Trumpet
 Mercury
Trundle bed
 Taurus
Trust
 11
Trust fund
 8
Truth
 Saturn, Jupiter
Tuberculosis
 6, Mercury, Gemini
Tuberculosis of the bone
 Capricorn
Tuesday
 Mars
Tumor
 Moon, Jupiter, Pluto, Cancer, Pisces
Tunis
 Cancer
Tunnel, underground
 Scorpio
Turbulence
 Mars, Uranus Turkey Virgo
Turkey (country)
 Virgo
Turmoil, inner or psychic
 12, Neptune
Turning point
 Square
Turquoise stone
 Mercury, Sagittarius, Aquarius
Turtle
 Moon, Pluto
Twin
 Gemini
Typewriter
 3, Mercury, Virgo
Typhoid
 Virgo

Typhus
 Scorpio
Typist
 3, 6, Mercury, Virgo
Tyrant
 Pluto

# U

Ulcer, stomach
 Cancer, Scorpio
Ulterior motive
 12, Neptune
Uncle, maternal
 12, Jupiter
Uncle, paternal
 5, Jupiter
Uncle
 6, Cancer
Uncle, illness of
 5
Uncommon pursuit
 Uranus
Under the earth
 4
Underground tunnel
 Scorpio
Under handedness
 4
Understanding
 Mercury, Pisces
Undertaker
 8, Saturn, Pluto, Scorpio
Underworld
 Pluto
Underworld character
 Pluto
Undeserved reward
 Jupiter
Undesignated other person
 7
Undisclosed condition
 12, Neptune
Undoing
 12, Neptune
Unearthing
 Pluto
Unemployment insurance
 6
Unexpected
 Uranus
Unexpected obstacle
 Uranus

Unforeseeable
 Uranus
Unforgiving
 Capricorn
Unfortunates
 12
Ungrateful
 Gemini
Uniformed worker
 Pluto
Uniform
 6, Jupiter
Union
 7
Union of two people
 7, Venus
Union, labor
 Aquarius
Unique expression
 Chiron
Unique thing
 Uranus
United States
 Gemini
United States political affairs
 Aquarius
University
 9, 12, Jupiter, Sagittarius
Unmarried individual
 Leo
Unpredictable
 Aquarius
Unrealistic
 Neptune
Unreality
 12, Neptune
Unseen
 12
Unsolved mystery
 Pisces
Unstable area
 Uranus
Unused area
 Saturn

Unusual happening
 Uranus
Unusual method
 11, Uranus
Unwilling conformity
 8, Pluto
Upheaval
 8, Pluto
Upholstery
 Libra
Upper class
 5, Sun
Upper Egypt
 Libra
Upper legislative house
 5
Upper level
 9, Jupiter
Upsets
 Uranus
Upsetting condition
 Saturn, Moon
Uranium
 Uranus, Aquarius
Urge for security
 Saturn, Moon
Urge to adapt to others
 7, Venus
Urination
 8
Usurer
 Mercury
Uterus
 Moon, Cancer
Utilities
 3
Utopian
 Uranus

*Astrological Keywords*

# V

Vacancy
  Pluto
Vacation
  5, Venus, Sun
Vacillation
  Moon, Mercury
Vagabond
  Moon
Vagina
  Scorpio
Vagrant
  9
Vagueness
  Neptune
Vain
  Leo
Valencia, Spain
  Scorpio
Valuables
  2, Venus, Jupiter
Valuable belonging to a querent
  Scorpio
Values
  2, Venus
Vandalism
  Neptune
Vanity
  5, Sun, Venus
Vapor
  Uranus
Varicose vein
  Aquarius
Vegetable garden
  Cancer
Vehicle body
  1
Vehicle, large
  Jupiter
Vehicle
  1, 3, Mercury, Uranus
Vehicle, garbage and rubbish
  Saturn
Vehicle, magnificent
  Sun

Vehicle, modern
  Neptune
Vehicle, small and light
  Mercury
Vehicle, speedy
  Uranus
Vehicle, used for everyday
  Gemini
Vein
  Venus, Jupiter
Vein in feet
  Pisces
Velvet
  Jupiter
Venereal disease
  8, Mars, Pluto, Scorpio, Pisces
Vengeful
  Scorpio
Venice
  Cancer
Ventilation
  3, Mercury, Uranus
Ventilator
  Aquarius
Venture
  1, Mars
Venture, new
  1, Mars, conjunction
Verbena herb
  Moon, Cancer
Verbosity
  Mercury
Verdict of the jury in court
  7
Vermin
  Pluto, Scorpio
Versatility
  Mercury
Vertebrae, cervical
  Taurus
Vertebrae, coccygeal
  Sagittarius
Vertebrae, lower lumbar
  Scorpio

Vertebrae, lumbar
  Libra
Vertigo
  Mercury, Aries
Veterinarian
  6, 12, Mercury, Virgo
Veterinary hospital
  Virgo
Vicarious experience
  11
Victim of a murder
  8
Victor in a battle
  7
Victory
  10
Vienna
  Libra
Vigor
  1, Mars
Village
  4
Vineyard
  Scorpio
Vintner
  Scorpio
Violence
  Mars
Violent
  Pluto, Aries, Scorpio
Violent crime
  8, Mars, Pluto
Virginia
  Virgo
Virgin
  Venus, Mercury
Virility
  Mars
Virtues, lasting
  Sagittarius
Virus
  Pluto
Visceral system
  Virgo

Astrological Keywords

Visible
　Aries
Vision
　9, 10
Visionary
　Neptune
Visitor
　3, Mercury
Visit
　3, Mercury
Vitality
　Mars
Vitamin
　6, Mercury
Vocal cords
　Venus, Taurus
Vocation
　10
Voice
　3
Voter in an election
　Moon
Voyage
　9, Moon, Jupiter
Vulture
　Pluto

# W

Wages
  2, 11
Wainscoting
  Gemini
Waiter
  6, Jupiter
Waitress
  6, Mercury
Wales
  Gemini
Wallet
  2, Venus
Wallpaper
  Gemini
Wall
  Saturn
Wall of house
  Gemini
Walnut Street
  Mercury
Wanderlust
  Moon, Neptune
War
  7, Mars, Pluto
Warden in a prison
  Saturn
Wardrobe
  5, Venus, Libra
Warehouse
  4
Warehouse for food
  Virgo
Warm-hearted
  Leo
Warmest part of the house
  5
Wart
  Jupiter
Washing machine
  Cancer, Moon, Neptune
Wasp
  Pluto
Waste and those who waste
  8, Pluto

Wasting disease
  Neptune
Watch
  Gemini
Watchman
  6
Water
  Moon
Water damage
  Neptune
Water power
  Neptune, Uranus
Water tank
  Neptune
Water, running
  Cancer
Water, salt
  Neptune, Pisces
Water, stagnant
  Scorpio
Water, standing
  Pisces
Water, healing
  Cancer
Waterfall
  Neptune, Saturn
Wealth
  2, Jupiter, Venus, Taurus
Wealth of father
  5
Wealth of marriage/business partner
  8
Wealth, great
  Pluto
Wealth, recovered
  4
Weapon
  Mars, Aries
Weapon, secret
  Scorpio
Weasel
  Pluto
Weather
  4, 6

Weather conditions along the coast
  9
Weather forecaster
  9
Weaving machine
  Virgo
Wedding
  9, Libra, Venus
Wedding announcement
  5
Wedding of a child
  1
Wednesday
  Mercury
Weighing machine
  Saturn
Weight
  Saturn
Welfare
  12, Neptune
Welfare agency
  12
Welfare funds
  Scorpio
Welfare program
  Neptune
Welfare recipient
  12
Welfare worker
  12, Jupiter
Well wishes
  11
Well being
  1, Sun
Well
  4, Pisces
West
  7, Libra
West Indies
  Virgo
West Pakistan
  Libra
Western Poland
  Aries

Astrological Keywords

Wet nurse
  Cancer
Whale
  Jupiter
What lasts
  9
What should be
  11
Whatever gratifies the senses
  Venus
Wheat
  Mercury
Wheelbarrow
  Saturn
Where living things grow
  4, Moon
Where you reflect or meditate
  Neptune
Where you reside
  4
Where you relocate to
  7
Whip
  Saturn, Mars
Whirlpool
  Uranus, Neptune
Whirlwind
  Mercury, Uranus
Whiskey
  Neptune
White
  Moon, Neptune, Pisces
White milk
  Moon, Aries, Cancer, Scorpio
Wholesaler
  Jupiter
Whooping cough
  Gemini, Mercury
Wider vision
  9
Widowhood
  12
Widow
  12, Saturn
Wife
  7, Moon, Venus
Wig
  Jupiter
Wild Beast
  Leo
Wilderness
  12
Wildlife preserve
  Leo
Willingness to gather experience
  Jupiter
Wills and legacies
  8
Wind damage
  Uranus
Windmill
  Neptune, Uranus
Window
  3
Wind
  Aquarius
Wind, circulation of
  Uranus
Wine, dry
  Sagittarius
Wine, fine
  Sun
Wine, heavy
  Jupiter
Wine merchant
  Scorpio
Wine, sweet
  Venus
Winnings
  9, Jupiter
Wireless
  Mercury, Gemini, 3rd
Wire
  Gemini
Wire, high powered
  Uranus
Wisdom
  9, Jupiter, Saturn, Chiron
Wisdom gained from experience
  Saturn
Wishes and hopes
  11, Aquarius, Uranus
Wit
  Mercury
Witchcraft
  12
Withdrawal into fantasy
  12
Witnesses
  3, Mercury
Wife
  7, Venus, Moon
Woman inquired about
  Moon
Womb
  4, Moon, Cancer, Taurus
Women
  Moon, Venus
Women in general
  Moon
Women's articles
  Venus
Women's clothing
  Venus
Women's liberation
  11, Uranus
Women, young
  Venus
Wood and wooden objects
  Libra
Wood pile
  Venus
Wood stove
  Sun
Wood, petrified
  Saturn
Wood, things made of
  Saturn
Wooded, hilly land
  Libra
Wool
  Saturn
Woolens
  Capricorn
Words
  3, Mercury
Work
  6, Saturn, Mercury, Mars
Work areas
  6, Mercury
Work behind the scenes
  12, Neptune
Work commonly avoided
  Saturn

Work done quietly or alone
    12, Neptune
Work habits
    6, Mercury
Work, hard
    Vesta
Work requiring wit or intelligent
    Mercury
Work room
    6
Work schedule
    6
Work with fire
    Mars
Work with heavy tools
    6
Work with iron or steel
    Mars
Work with liquids
    Moon, Neptune
Work with oil
    Neptune
Work with sharp instruments
    Mars
Worker
    6, Mercury
Worker at routine job for wages
    6, Mercury
Worker in any trade
    6, Mercury
Working class
    6, Mercury
Working conditions
    6
Working environment
    6, Mercury
Workmen's Compensation
    6, 8
Workshop
    6
World assemblies like the UN
    9
World view
    9, Jupiter, Aquarius
World wide contacts
    9, Jupiter
Worldly position
    10, Sun, Saturn

Worm
    Virgo
Wormwood herb
    Mars, Scorpio
Worries
    12, Saturn
Worth
    2
Worship, places of
    Jupiter
Wounds
    8, Mars, Aries, Gemini
Wrestling match
    Scorpio
Wrist
    Leo, Gemini
Writer
    3, Mercury, Neptune, Gemini
Writing
    Mercury
Writing, gain from
    4
Writing skills
    3, Mercury
Writing talent
    Mercury
Writing tools
    Mercury, Gemini
Writings
    3, Mercury
Written document
    3, Mercury
Written test
    3

# X

X-ray
　11, Uranus, Aquarius
X-ray technician
　6

# Y

Yacht
: Neptune, Moon

Yam
: Capricorn

Yard
: 4

Yeast
: Neptune, 7

Yellow fever
: Leo

Yesterday
: 12, Saturn

Yoga
: Neptune, 7

Yoke
: 7, Venus, Saturn

Young girl
: Venus

Young man
: Mars

Young people
: Mercury, Venus

Young person, dealing with
: 5

Young woman
: Venus

Youngster
: Moon

Youth
: Mercury

Yugoslavia
: Sagittarius

# Z

Zinc mine
  Capricorn
Zinc, anything made from
  Capricorn
Zoo
  6, 12, Jupiter, Uranus, Leo

# Keywords for Signs

# Aries

Acne
Activity
Acute fever
Adrenal
Amethyst stone
Animal stable, small animal
Arrogance
Bandleader
Baron land
Blacksmith
Bleeding, excessive
Bloodstain
Bloodstone stone
Boil down
Borage herb
Brain
Broccoli
Brusque
Cayenne herb
Ceiling and plaster walls
Ceiling
Cerebral hemorrhage
Cerebral congestion
Cerebrum
Competitive
Contest
Courageous
Criminal
Cut
Dawn of a new day
Day, new
Denmark
Desert
Diamond stone
Domineering
Dry pasture
Dwelling, temporary
Dynamic
Eager
Early morning
Egotistic
England
Epilepsy

Executive
Explorer
Eye problem
Eye
Eyebright herb
Face
Fever
Fish
Fugitive, hiding place
Furnace
Garnet stone
Germany
Hasty
Head of the body
Headache
Hernia
Hiding place for fugitives
Hops herb
Hunter
Impetuou
Impulsive
Independent
Inflammation
Initiator
Insomnia
Intolerance
Iron
Italy from Naples south
Jasper stone
Jaw, upper
Kiln
Knives and sharp instruments
Lack follow-through
Land, eroded
Land, recently cleared
Leader
Lives in the present
Malachite stone
Migraine
Milk, white
Mustard seeds
Neuralgia
Nomad
Object, broken

Object made of iron or steel
Outspoken
Palestine
Pasture, dry
Pea
Peppermint herb
Pioneer
Pioneering
Place unfrequented or unexplored
Plastering, in home
Poland, east
Positive
Provocative
Rash
Rebel
Rebellion
Restless
Rhubarb
Ringworm
Roof
Rude
Rupture
Scarlet fever
Sensual
Sheep
Sheep farmer
Sheepherder
Smallpox
Soldier
Spice, strong like pepper
Spontaneous
Stable for small animals
Starter
Steel
Syria
Teeth, upper
Temper, quick
Tent
To dare
Tomato
Vertigo
Violent weapon
Visible
Western Poland

Wound

# Taurus

Abscess
Accident to throat or neck
Acquire
Alabaster stone
Almond
Apoplexy
Apple
Architect
Argumentative
Asia minor
Avocado
Banana
Bank
Banker
Barn, dairy
Basement
Bean
Beheading
Bird, song
Blackcurrant herb
Blood, impure
Bronze
Bronze, objects made of
Bull ring
Cattle breeder
Cattle
Cellar
Cerebellum
Cervical vertebrae
Change, slow
Chimney
Choir
Choking
Cloves herb
Clumsy
Cold
Color, cream
Color, red-orange
Color, blue
Color, yellow
Color, brown
Color, red
Conservative
Copper metal
Cottage
Cowboy
Cyprus
Dairy barn
Dairy equipment
Dairy farmer
Dependable
Determined
Diphtheria
Ear
Eastern Poland
Emerald stone
Esophagus, upper part
Eustachian tube
Fair
Fallow
Fertile
Field
Field of grain
Follow through, lacking
Footstool
Glee club
Goiter
Granary
Grape
Greedy
Ground, close to
Hanging
Horse stable
House, low in the country
Idealistic
Indecision
Insurance broker
Ireland
Jade
Jaw, lower
Lapis lazuli stone
Laryngitis
Larynx
Lazy
Lovage herb
Loyal
Materialistic
Melancholy
Money
Money belonging to querent
Moneylender
Moss-agate stone
Neck
Obesity
Object placed under thing
Pastures, fertile
Patient
Persia
Pharynx
Plow
Poland, east
Possess
Possessive
Practical
Property
Purse
Quiet
Respond
Road builder
Room, low
Russia, Southern
Safe
Safe deposit box
Sage herb
Sculptor
Self-indulgent
Sensual
Singer
Slow-moving
Sorrel herb
Southern Russia
Spearmint herb
Speech, slow
Stable hand
Stable
Stable for horses
Strangulation
Stubborn
Sunflower herb
Thorough
Throat specialist

*Astrological Keywords*

Throat, sore
Throat, accident or wound to
Throat
Thyroid
Tonsillitis
Tonsils
Trundle bed
Valuable belonging to the querent
Vertebrate, cervical
Vocal cords
Wealth

# Gemini

- Accident
- Adaptable
- Agate stone
- Airplane
- Anemia
- Aniseed herb
- Appliance, small
- Aquamarine stone
- Arm of the body
- Asthma
- Balm herb
- Barn, airy
- Beryl stone
- Bicycle
- Bird, small
- Blood, impure
- Book
- Bookshelf
- Box
- Bronchitis
- Bus
- Capillary
- Car
- Caraway herb
- Cards, playing
- Carrot
- Cauliflower
- Change, quick
- Changeable
- Cheese
- Chess
- Chest, high
- Childlike
- Chrysolite stone
- Clever
- Color, orange
- Color, piebald
- Color, blue
- Color, violet
- Comedian
- Communicating
- Commuting
- Concentration, lack of
- Congenial
- Connecting
- Connection
- Conversation
- Corn crib
- Crystal
- Curious
- Delusion
- Democratic
- Desk
- Dexterous
- Document Belgium
- Dominoes
- Door to door salesman
- Dual
- Egypt, lower
- Elementary school
- Email
- Emphysema
- England, west of
- Expressive
- Fickle
- Flighty
- Forger
- Gadget
- Game room
- Garlic
- Gossip
- Hall in house
- Hallucination
- Hand wound
- Hands and arms
- Hill
- House wall
- Idea
- Idealistic
- Inquiry
- Intellectual
- Inventive
- Inventor
- Italy, northeastern
- Knick knack
- Lack follow through
- Land, well drained
- Land, open
- Lavender herb
- Lecturer
- Letter
- Lettuce
- Liar
- Liberty loving
- Lien
- Literary
- London
- Lung
- Magazine
- Manuscript
- Marble stone
- Marjoram herb
- Mathematician
- Measuring device
- Mental illness
- Mental
- Mercury metal
- Messenger
- Mimic
- Monkey
- Mountain
- Neighbor
- Nerve illness
- Nervous disease
- Nervous
- Newspaper
- Nimble
- Nursery
- Parsley herb
- Phone
- Pickpocket
- Playground
- Pleurisy
- Pneumonia
- Quick-witted
- Reporter
- Research
- Respiration
- Restlessness
- Ribs, upper
- Rumor

Salesperson, door to door
Scatterbrained
Scheming
Scholar
School, elementary
Science
Scientist
Searching
Speech
Study
Suburb
Talkative
Teacher, elementary and high school
Teaching
Telephone
Tennis court
Thermometer
Thermostat
Thief
Thinking
Thoughts
Thymus gland
Tic, uncontrollable
Tobacco barn
Tool shed
Topaz stone
Trader
Tremors and tics
Trip, short
Tuberculosis
Twins
Ungrateful
United States
Vehicle used for everyday
Wainscoting
Wall of house
Wallpaper
Watch
Whaler
Wire
Wound
Writer
Writing tools

# Cancer

- Africa, north and west
- Alimentary system
- Allergy
- Amphibious creatures
- Amsterdam
- Animal, newborn
- Armpit
- Asthma
- Balm herb
- Bar, tavern
- Bartender
- Bathroom
- Beach
- Bird, water
- Boat
- Breast cancer
- Breast
- Bronchitis
- Brooding
- Brook
- Cabbage
- Canal
- Cancer, breast, stomach, uterus
- Caregiver
- Castle
- Cautious, overly
- Cave
- Cellar, underground
- Charitable organization that feeds people
- Charity, organizer
- Chemist, organic
- Childbirth
- Childhood disease
- Cistern
- Color, blue-green
- Color, orange-yellow
- Constantinople
- Cook
- Cough
- Crystal stone
- Diaphragm
- Digestive disorder
- Diphtheria
- Disease caused by emotional problems
- Disease of childhood
- Ditch
- Domestic worker
- Domestic
- Domestic worker
- Dropsy
- Egg
- Embryo
- Emerald stone
- Emotion
- Emotional
- Emotional problem
- Epigastric region
- Experiencing
- Family
- Feeling
- Fern
- Fish
- Flatulence
- Gardener
- Genoa
- Grotto
- Gynecologist
- Healing waters
- Health, poor, especially in childhood
- Helpful
- Holland
- Home loving
- Home
- House, developer
- Housekeeper
- Hurt easily
- Hypochondriac
- Incubator
- Infant
- Inflammatory disease
- Intuitive
- Kidney trouble
- Kitchen
- Laboratory
- Laboratory technician
- Lacteal
- Lake
- Land, fertile
- Land bordering water
- Land with a pond, brook, spring, or well
- Landlord
- Laundry room
- Lazy
- Liver, upper lobes
- Manchester, England
- Manipulation of others
- Marsh
- Maternal
- Memory, good
- Menstrual disorder
- Milan
- Mother hen
- Mother
- Nest
- Netherlands
- New York
- New Zealand
- Newborn animal
- North
- Nourishment
- Nurse, wet
- Nursery person
- Object made of silver
- Onyx, black stone
- Organic chemist
- Ovarian trouble
- Pancreas
- Paraguay
- Patient
- Patriotic
- Pearl stone
- Pediatrics
- Plumbing
- Poliomyelitis
- Pregnancy
- Provider
- Psychological problems

*Astrological Keywords*

Pumps
Real estate
Real estate developer
Reeds, where they grow
Restaurant
Retentive
River
Russian Georgia
Sailor
Saxifrage herb
Scoliosis
Scotland
Sea
Security
Selenite stone
Selfish
Sensitive
Sensitivity
Ship's hold
Shy
Silver object
Silver metal
Solar plexus
Sorry for self
Spa
Spinach
Spring
Stomach
Stomach cancer
Stomach problem
Sweets, over consumption of
Sympathetic
Tangerine
Tarragon herb
Tenacious
Thoracic duct
Touchy
Traditional
Tumor
Tunis
Ulcer, stomach
Uterus, cancer
Vegetable garden
Venice
Verbena herb
Washing machine
Water, running
Wet nurse
White milk

Womb

# Leo

Actor
Aggressive
Alps, the
Amateur love action
Ambassador
Ambitious
Amusement, owner of place of
Angelica herb
Angina pectoris
Animal, wild
Appliance that produces heat
Arena, owner of
Arena
Art object
Artery
Artist
Artistic
Athletic coach
Autocratic
Back, upper
Back, wound to
Beast, wild
Beekeeper
Bird, fancy plumage
Boasting
Body, side of
Bohemia
Bohemian
Boxer
Building, government
Carbuncle stone
Castle
Cauliflower
Cheese
Chicago
Childish
Children
Chimney
Cholera
Circulation, poor
Circus performer
Circus
Coach, athletic

Color, yellow
Color, orange
Color, gold
Color, red
Confident
Coronary thrombosis
Creative
Crown
Cruel
Dandelion herb
Diamond stone
Dignified
Director, theatrical
Drama
Dramatic
Dramatist
Education, secondary school
Expressive
Eye infection or injurie
Eyebright herb
Fainting
Fear of ridicule
Fever
Fever, dangerously high
Firefighter
Fireplace
Forest
Forester
Fort
France
Fur
Gallbladder
Game meat
Game warden
Generous
Gold metal
Gold, item of
Goldsmith
Gypsy
Heart palpitation
Heart
Heart specialist
Heart, malfunction of
Hearth

Hobby
Hobbyist
Honey
Honeybee
Host of a party
Hotel
Hunter
Hunting gear
Hunting parks or grounds
Hyacinth stone
Idealistic
Italy
Jewelry, precious
Jungle
King
Lamp
Land, inaccessible places
Land, hunting
Lovers
Meat, game
Meat
Museum
Northeast
Optimistic
Ostentatious item
Outgoing
Oven
Overbearing
Palpitations
Park
Pea
Peppermint herb
Pestilence
Philadelphia
Physical
Place
Plague
Prague
Pretentious
Prideful
Prince
Producer, theatrical
Proud
Prune

Astrological Keywords

Queen
Recuperation, powers of
Rib
Romantic
Rome
Rosemary herb
Ruby stone
Saffron herb
School, secondary
Self-assured
Sicily
Side, wound to
Speculation
Speculator
Spinach
Spinal meningitis
Spinal cord
Spinal column
Sports
Stage
Status conscious
Stock exchange
Stockbroker
Stove
Teacher
Theater
Theater, owner of
Theatrical costume
Theatrical
Theatrical producer or director
Tiger eye stone
Toy
Trapper of large wild animal
Treasurer
Unmarried individual
Vain
Warm-hearted
Wild beast
Wildlife preserve
Wound to back or side
Yellow fever
Zoo

# Virgo

Agate stone
Agent
Alfalfa
Alimentary canal
Allergy, food
Analyze
Animal as pet
Animal hospital
Anxious
Appendicitis
Aquamarine stone
Armed forces, member of
Baghdad
Bookkeeper
Bookkeeping office
Books, accounting
Bowel, upper
Carbuncle stone
Careful
Cat
Cheese
Cholera
Civil service
Clean
Clockmaker
Closets
Clover
Color, blue
Color, violet
Color, yellow
Color, yellow-green
Compassionate caring
Computer programmer
Computer
Concern/worry
Conservation
Conserving
Cookbook
Cotton
Crete
Critical
Cupboard
Cupboard

Den
Details
Diet
Diet deficiency
Diet deficiency disease
Dietitian
Digestion
Digestion, process of
Digestive disorder
Dill herb
Discriminating
Disease and poverty
Disease, fear of
Diverticulitis
Drugstore
Duodenum Brazil
Dysentery Cabinets
Eating, fussy
Employee
Epidemic
Exacting
Fact-finding
Fears
Fennel herb
Field of grain
Fighter
Functional item
Fussing
Gallbladder
Gastroenteritis
Germs and infections, fearful of
Granary
Greece
Grocery store
Hay
Health, overly concerned with
Health, poor
Heidelberg
Herb
Homeopathic physician
Hospital, animal
Housekeeper, compulsive
Humane
Hyacinth stone

Hypochondriac
Indies, West
Industrious
Intestinal parasites
Intestines
Intestines, obstruction of
Jasper stone
Jerusalem
Land, field of grain, hay, alfalfa
Ledger
Lemon
Librarian
Literary agent
Liver
Liver, lower lobes
Liverpool
Lyons
Malnutrition
Marble stone
Medicine chest
Medicine
Melancholy
Mesopotamia
Methodical
Mind overly preoccupied with body
Mouse
Nurse
Office worker
Orange
Pancreas
Pantry
Paris
Parsley herb
Peach
Pedantic
Perfection, seek
Peritonitis
Pet
Petty
Pharmacist
Physician, homeopathic
Picky
Pocket
Posture, poor

Astrological Keywords

Poultry
Poverty, fear of
Precise
Printer
Property, profitable
Property, dreary
Prunes
Restaurant
Rooming house
Scientific
Secretary
Self-analytical
Self-centered
Servant quarters
Serving others
Shelf for food
Shop clerk
Silo
Skeptical
Sloppy
Solar plexus
Spider
Spinster
Spleen
Studious
Study
Switzerland
Tailor
Tapeworm
Tenant/lodger
Textile worker
Thoughtful
Topaz stone
Travel agent
Turkey
Turkey, the country
Typewriter
Typhoid
Typist
Veterinarian
Veterinary hospital
Virginia
Visceral system
Warehouse for food
Weaving machine
West Indies
Worm

# Libra

Adrenal gland
Alabaster stone
Ally
Antwerp
Apartment, luxury
Apathetic
Appendix
Argentina
Art dealer
Art museum
Artist
Artistic
Asparagus
Attic
Austria
Back, weakness
Back, lower
Backache
Beauty parlor
Bedroom
Beryl stone
Burma
Carnelian stone
Carpenter
Caspian Sea, area near
Charleston, South Carolina
Chest top
China
Chrysolite stone
Clothing, fashionable
Clothing model
Color, green
Color, white
Color, pastel
Color, coral
Color, crimson
Companionable
Cooperative
Copper, thing made of
Copper, metal
Coppersmith
Coral stone
Cosmetician
Cosmetics
Counselor, marriage
Courthouse
Criminal lawyer
Cupboard, high
Dancing teacher
Date, fruit
Diabetics
Diplomatic
Divorce lawyer
Dress designer
Easily deterred
Egypt, upper
Elegant house
Equality based
Fabric, elegant
Fair
Falcon
Fickle
Flower garden
Forester
Forum
Frankfurt
Furniture factory
Garden, flower
General
Gravel and sand pits
Hairdresser
Hillside
Hilltop
Horseradish
House, elegant
Hunting ground for birds
Impersonal
Indecisive
India, northern
Interior decorator
Jade stone
Japan
Jewelry store
Judicial
Kidney trouble
Kidney
Lace
Land, sandy
Land, wooded hilly land
Lapis lazuli stone
Lawyer, criminal
Lawyer, divorce
Legal partnership
Lisbon
Loins
Loves intrigue
Lumbago
Lumbar vertebrae
Lumber yard
Luxury building
Marriage counselor
Marriage
Model, clothing
Moss-agate stone
Mushroom
Object, copper
Object, wooden
Opal stone
Orange
Outbuilding
Ovary
Pakistan, west
Parsley herb
Partner
Partnership, legal
Peace loving
Peace at any price
Peace
Perfume
Persuasive
Poultry to eat
Pouting
Public face
Public enemy
Raisin
Refined
Renal system
Responsible
Responsive
Rooms inside another
Rooms, upper

Sawmill
Skin
Sociable
Social
Solon
South Carolina
Spinal trouble
Strategist
Strategy
Suave
Sweets, addiction to
Thyme herb
Tibet
Tobacco barn
Town squares Museums, fine art
Treaty
Upholstery
Upper Egypt
Vertebrae, lumbar
Vienna
Wardrobe
West
Wood and wooden objects
Wooded and wooden objects
Wooded, hilly land

# Scorpio

- Abandoned house
- Algeria
- Annuity
- Anus
- Archaeologist
- Archaeology
- Aware
- Barbary Coast
- Barracuda
- Basil herb
- Bavarian
- Bird of prey
- Bladder
- Bladder disorder
- Bloodstone stone
- Bowel, lower
- Brothel owner
- Brothel
- Budapest
- Buried treasure
- Business
- Butcher
- Butcher shop
- Castration
- Catalonia, Spain
- Cauliflower
- Celibate
- Cesaerean
- Clam
- Colon
- Color, greenish blue
- Color, red murky
- Color, brown
- Creature, dangerous sea
- Death
- Debt
- Detectives
- Determined
- Dictatorship
- Disease caused by insect
- Drain
- Drawer, secret
- Elimination, process of
- Excess, getting rid of
- Executioner
- Executive
- Fierce
- Flint stone
- Fruit grower
- Gang, street
- Gangster
- Garden
- Genitals
- Ghetto
- Ginseng herb
- Gonorrhea
- Groin
- Ground, muddy
- Gynecologist
- Haunted house
- Hemorrhoid
- Hernia
- Hidden place
- Horse, fall from a
- House, decaying
- House, vandalized
- House, abandoned
- Hysterectomy
- Infection caused by vermin
- Inheritance
- Insurance broker
- Intense
- Intolerant
- Investigative
- Iron, scrap
- Jasper stone
- Jealousy
- Judo
- Junk dealer
- Junkyard
- Lake, stagnant or polluted
- Land in danger of flooding
- Land, muddy
- Land, slum property
- Land, swampy
- Latrine
- Lemon
- Lobster
- Lodestone stone
- Lumbar vertebrae, lower
- Malachite stone
- Maroon
- Mausoleum
- Mercenary soldier
- Milwaukee
- Mine
- Morgue
- Morocco
- Motivated
- Nasal bone
- Naval officer
- Negotiations, secret
- Nitty gritty
- Northeast
- Norway
- Nuclear physicist
- Octopus
- Orchard
- Organize crime
- Overbearing
- Oyster
- Parsley herb
- Passionate
- Peach
- Pelvis
- Penetrating
- Penis
- Pension
- Personal
- Philanderer
- Pimp
- Piracy
- Pirate
- Place secret or hidden
- Privy
- Probing
- Prostate gland
- Prostitute
- Prostitution
- Prune
- Psychiatrist

Astrological Keywords

Pubic bone
Quicksand
Rat
Rectum
Red tape, no
Removing obstacle
Reproductive organ
Research scientist
Resourceful
Rheumatism
Room, damp
Ruins
Rupture
Sailor
Sarcastic
Sciatica
Scientific research
Scientific
Scientist, research
Scrap iron
Scurvy
Secret place
Secretive
Sewer
Sex organ
Sex
Sexual
Shark
Shrimp
Sink
Slaughterhouse
Slum property
Snake bite
Social worker
Soldier, mercenary
Stomach ulcer
Suspicious
Swine
Syphilis
Taxes
Temperamental
Testicle
Toilet
Tomb
Topaz stone
Treasure, buried
Tunnel, underground
Typhus
Ulcer, stomach

Underground tunnel
Undertaker
Vagina
Valencia, Spain
Valuables, places used to hide
Venereal disease
Vengeful
Vermin
Vertebrae, lower lumbar
Vineyard
Vintner
Violate
Water, stagnant
Weapon, secret
Welfare funds
Wine merchant

# Sagittarius

Amethyst stone
Archery
Argumentative
Asparagus
Athletics
Australia
Balcony
Bay herb
Blunt
Bridge, high
Broad-minded
Broadcaster
Broadcasting, commercial
Burn
Buttocks
Candid
Carbuncle stone
Cathedral
Ceiling, close to
Clergy
Clown
Coccygeal vertebrae
Cologne, city of
Color, blue
Color, red
Color, yellow
Color, yellow-green
Color, chartreuse
Commercial broadcasting
Counselor to king or president
Courtroom
Cucumber
Diplomat
Direct
Education, higher
Egg
Enthusiasm
Equality-minded
Ethics
Even-handedness
Exaggerative
Explorer
Fair
Fire, forest
Foreign policy of a country
Foreign correspondence
Foreign correspondent
Foreign country
Foreign policy
Foreign service
Forest fire
Freedom loving
Gambler
Gambling
Generous
Glass
Gout
Harsh
Heat exhaustion
Hepatic system
Hips
Homes where clergy live
Horse
Horse breeder
Horse, fall from
Horse gear
Horse pasture
Horse racing
Horse trainer
Hothead
House with extensive grounds
Hungary
Hunter, big game
Hunting injury
Hunting park or grounds
Hunting expedition
Hyacinth stone
Impatient
Import business
Importer
Jockey
Journey, long
Land, pasture for horses
Land, open hilly
Land, highest
Law, codes of
Lawyer
Lawyer's office
Leg, upper
Lottery
Malaria
Mansion/estate, great
Metal, tin
Moonstone stone
Morality
Mountain climber
Mountain climbing
Mountaintop
Object made from tin
Optimistic
Overexposure to heat
Pasture for horses
Pea
Philanderer
Philosopher
Philosophical
Philosophy
Procrastination
Public relations
Publisher
Publisher's office
Publishing
Pumpkin seed
Pushy
Race track
Racing stables
Religion
Religious artifact
Religious
Riding school
Room, upper
Safari
Satirist
Scholar
Scholarly
School, riding
Sciatic nerve
Sciatica
Self-indulgence
Seminary
Skyscraper

Snakebite
Spain
Spinach
Spirituality
Stables, racing
Straightforward
Sunstroke
Talkative
Thigh
Tin metal
Toledo, Spain
Topaz stone
Traveler, world
Trip, long or distant
Truthful
Turquoise stone
University
Vertebrae, coccygeal
Virtue, lasting
Yugoslavia

# Capricorn

Administrator, estate
Albania
Appraising
Armor
Arthritis
Barn for farm machinery
Barren land
Belts
Bone
Bone, broken
Bone surgeon
Border between countries or states
Bosnia
Boundary line
Boundary
Bricklayer
Brooding
Building, functional
Buildings, commercial
Bulgaria
Business
Business manager
Businesslike
Calcium deficiency disease
Camphor herb
Carrot
Cask, wooden
Cautious
Cement worker
Chains
Chronic invalid
Clear-headed
Coal
Coal miner
Color, black
Color, indigo
Color, gray
Color, blue violet
Color, somber
Comfrey herb
Commercial building
Compost heap
Confine and protect

Confines, anything that
Contractor of large functional
    buildings
Conventional
Cool
Cord
Corner, dark
Corporation
Country
Court, night
Court, probate
Court magistrate
Cramps
Crow
Crutches
Custom official
Customs fees and tariffs
Dark corner
Dark place
Deafness
Dermatitis
Dermatologist
Dessert
Detailed
Diamond merchant
Diamond mine
Diamond miner
Diamond stone
Discipline, those who enforce
Domineering
Door
Economical
Eczema
Egotistic
Epidermis, outer
Estate of the dead
Estate administrator
Executive
Fatalistic
Father
Funeral
Fur
Garment bag, leather
Gate

Goat shed
Goat
Governor
Gray
Greece
Hair
Hard-working
Health, poor
Heart is ruled by mind
Hide of animal
India
Inhibited
Invalid, chronic
Iran, part of
Jet stone
Judge, probate
Jury room
Knee
Land, barren field
Land, unused
Lead
Lead, anything may of
Lead mine
Leather worker
Lens grinder
Leprosy
Lithuania
Liver to eat
Lock
Locksmith
Logical
Luggage
Magistrate in court
Management
Manager, business
Manure pile
Mayor
Mexico
Mind rules heart
Miser
Moonstone stone
Mourning clothing
Old
Onyx, white stone

Astrological Keywords

Orkney Islands
Orthopedic equipment
Osteomyelitis
Overseeing
Oxford
Panama
Parsley herb
Passport
Perfectionist
Police officer
Police station
Pottery
Practical
Practical sense
Principal, school
Probate court
Probate judge
Protect and confine
Psoriasis
Railroad
Railroad worker
Raven
Real estate
Responsible
Rheumatism
Rickets
Rope
Saddle
Sail maker
Sail
Sapphire stone
Saxony
School principal
Scrupulous
Scurvy
Seaweed
Serious
Shoe store or factory
Skeleton
Skin condition
Skin
Slate stone
Slum
South
Spine, curvature of the
Stable for work animals
Status seeking
Stone
Stone quarry

Stonemasons
String
Stubborn
Tannery
Tariff
Teeth
Threshold
Timber lands, cut
Tomato
Traditional
Trucker
Tuberculosis of the bone
Unforgiving
Wood, rare
Woolen
Yam
Zinc, anything made of
Zinc mine

# Aquarius

Adopted children
Adoption
Afghanistan
Air conditioning unit
Aircraft
Airline
Altruistic
Aluminum metal
Ankle
Ankle, sprained, swollen, or broken
Antique collector
Antique
Apartment on upper floor
Aquamarine stone
Arabia
Arabian desert
Archaeological digging
Artistic
Assembly
Astronautics
Astronomy
Aviation
Aviator
Balcony, high
Balcony
Balloon
Bean
Belfry
Berlin
Blood poisoning
Book, old
Bored by detail
Bremen
Broccoli
Calves of the body
Chalcedony stone
Cheese
Child, adopted
Circulatory disorder
Civil rights
Cloud
Clubhouse for public meeting
Clubhouse
Co-op
Cold temperament
Collector of antiques
Color, indigo
Color, violet
Community-minded
Corporate reorganization
Cramp, leg
Demonstration, street
Disease of the blood stream
Eave
Eccentric
Elected representative
Election
Electioneering
Electronics
Elk
England, political affairs
Epilepsy
Fish
Fixed in opinion
Fraternal organization
Future-minded
Garden, roof
Group work
Hamburger, Germany
Honey
House, modern
Human blood, circulation of
Hurricane
Impartial
Impersonal
Independent
Individualistic
Intellectual
Inventive
Kite
Labor organizer
Labor union
Land, hilly and windswept
Land, freshly plowed field
Land, newly excavated
Leg, crippling
Leg weakness
Leg, knee to ankle
Leg, lower
Leg cramp
Leukemia
Life, etheric vibration of
Lightning rod
Logical
Mason
Mass marketing, people engaged in
Merger
Moscow
Nerve network
Non-sectarian
Northwest
Office on upper floor
Opal stone
Organization, fraternal
Outer space
Parliament
Penthouse
People, eccentric
Physicist
Physics
Planner
Poland, parts bordering on Prussia
Political affairs of the United States
Political affairs of England
Political orator
Progressive
Prussia
Public meeting hall
Public relations worker
Quarry
Radiation poisoning
Radical
Radio commentator
Radio and entertainment
Radio technician
Radio
Radio as communication
Radioactivity
Radium
Rebellion
Reorganization

Astrological Keywords

Reorganization of corporation
Revolution
Revolutionary
Riot
Roof
Rotary club
Russia
Sapphire stone
Science of astrology
Scientific
Shin
Shy
Skin
Slate stone
Social experiment
Social theory
Sociologist
Sociology
Space research
Spinach
Sweden
Sweden, lower
Teeth
Telegraph
Temperamental
Thermodynamics
Tibet
Tolerant
Turquoise stone
Union, labor
United States political affairs
Unpredictable
Uranium
Varicose vein
Ventilator
Wind
World view

# Pisces

Accepting
Agent, secret
Alcoholic
Alcoholism
Amethyst stone
Artistic
Ballet
Bergtamont herb
Birth injury due to delivery
Birth defect due to drug use
Birth deformity
Bondage, those in
Building, condemned
Bunion
Color, gray-green
Cancer
Cereal
Charitable
Chemical
Chemist
Children, illegitimate
Christianity
Chrysolite stone
Clairvoyant
Cold
Color, blue
Color, green
Color, white
Color, violet-red
Compassionate
Concentration camp
Convent
Criminal hangout
Dancer
Date fruit
Deep
Discarded thing
Disease, genetically transmitted
Diver
Dreams and visions
Drug addict
Drug pusher
Drug addiction
Drugs
Dungeon
Duodenum
Egg
Emotional
Emotionally inhibited
Emotions, feel misunderstood
Enemy, secret
Exploited, those who are
Fig
Fish
Fish pond
Fisher
Fog
Foot, vein in
Foot deformity
Foot, damage to
Foot
Forgiving
Foundling
Galicia, Spain
Genetically transmitted disease
Ghetto
Ghost
Gout
Hallucination
Health, poor
Heart, malfunction of
Hemophilia
Hepatitis
Hyacinth stone
Illness due to damp cold
Impractical
Indecisive
Indolent
Insane asylum
Introspection
Intuitive
Jail
Junk dealer
Junkyard
Karma
Kelp
Land, swampy
Land likely to flood
Liquor
Liver
Liver disease
Long suffering
Lung trouble
Mammal of the sea
Martyrdom
Melancholy
Mind, subconscious
Moat
Molasses
Monastery
Monk
Moonstone stone
Motion picture
Mucous discharge
Musical
Mystery, unsolved
Mysticism
Neighborhood, declining
Neurotic
Normandy
Northwest
Noxious fumes
Nun
Occultism
Ocean
Oil
Orphanage
Patience
Penal colony
Pessimism
Photography
Piracy
Pituitary gland
Poison
Poisoning
Portugal
Prison
Prison camp
Prisoner
Procrastinating
Psychic phenomenon

Psychoanalyst
Psychological
Pus discharge
Raisin
Real estate, caution in matter of
Retirement, place of
River
Sacrificing
Sailor
Scavenger
Sea
Seashore
Secret agent
Self-sacrificing
Sickle cell anemia
Slave
Slave quarters
Sleep
Slum
Stockade
Suicide
Swamp
Sympathetic
Talkative, overly
Tidal basin
Timid
Title, clouded property
Toe
Toe deformity
Topaz stone
Trash heap
Tumor
Understanding
Unsolved mystery
Vein in foot
Venereal disease
Water, standing
Well

# Keywords for Houses

# First House

Accident, liability
Accident
Action
Activity
Adventurer
Aggressor
Ambitions
Appearance
Arrival
Beginning of any enterprise
Beginning of life
Beginnings, new
Birth
Bodily well-being
Body
Body of a vehicle
Brain
Childhood environment
Childhood, early
Color, white
Death of a pet
Debut
Decision of a court in a lawsuit
Desire for action
Disposition, natural
End of career matter
End of tenth house parent
Façade
Face
Focus of things
General well-being
Grandfather (maternal)
Grandmother (paternal)
Grandparent
Great grandchildren
Group acting as an entity
Head of body
Health
Home team
How others see an individual
Impression one makes on others
Individualism
Individualistic
Initiation of project
Initiative
Investment, sound
Launching
Leadership
Length of life
Life of man
Mind, state of
Nephew by marriage
Newcomer
Niece by marriage
Outlook, worldly
Person, absent and not related to querent
Person, absent
Personal interests
Personal prowess
Personal appearance
Personality
Physical body
Pioneer
Place where querent spends most of the time
Project, new emergence
Querent
Self
Self-assertion
Self-confidence
Selfhood
Ship at sea
Sorrows, secret
Spark of life
Start of a cycle
Surface
Temperament
Thing one begins
Travel of children
Vehicle
Venture, new
Vigor
Wedding of a child
Well-being

# Second House

Ability to handle funds
Acquire, how one does
Advancement, economic
Ancestor
Asset, tangible
Asset, negotiable
Asset, liquid or monetary
Bank account
Banker
Belongings
Bill
Bonds and securities
Budget
Buying and selling
Career of child
Cash at hand
Cash flow
Cash register
Chattel
Checkbook
Checking account
Clothing and possessions
Coin
Custom
Death of someone inquired about
Death of another
Ear
Earning capacity
Earnings
Economic outlook
Economy
Finances
Financial obligations of the querent
Financial transaction
Financial matter
Financial assistance
Financial settlement
Future
Future, immediate
Gift one gives
Home life
Income, ability to increase
Income, effort to increase
Income
Investment, not speculative
Investment
Investor
Jewelry as wealth
Loss or damage
Loss, financial
Loss or gain
Lost items in general
Loves, how one
Mislaid item
Missing thing
Money others owe the querent
Money, place where kept
Money, spending
Money
Movable possessions
Neck
Personal finances
Personal wealth
Personal property
Personal belongings
Pocketbook
Possession, movable
Profit or gain
Property, movable
Property
Resources, personal
Responds, how one
Response
Riches
Rights
Royalty
Safe
Safe-deposit box
Salary
Savings
Secret of a sibling
Securities, negotiable
Securities
Security
Self-worth
Singer
Stolen thing
Substance
Supplies for consumption
Talent
Tangible asset
Throat
Trade
Valuable
Values
Wages
Wallet
Wealth
Worth

# Third House

Accident
Accuracy
Ad writer
Adaptability
Advertisement (written copy)
Advertiser
Agent
Agreement (written document)
Anonymous
Arm of body
Automobile
Bicycle
Book
Box
Breathing
Brother
Bus
Bus driver
Camera
Car
Car repair
Clerk
Cleverness
Close relative
Collarbone
Color, yellow
Comings and goings
Communication
Communication, skill at
Commuter
Commuting
Computer
Computer technician
Conference, large meeting
Connecting things
Connections
Container
Contract, signing of
Contract, written document
Conversation
Conveyance
Correspondence
Coupon
Court reporter

Cousins, generic
Daily comings and goings
Dealer
Decisions
Deed, written
Delivery person
Delivery
Desk
Diary
Discussion
Document
Driving test
Driving
Editor and editing
Education
Education, elementary
Education, lower
Educational advancement
Email
Environment in general
Errand
Examination, oral or written
Exploration
File cabinet
Finger
Friend
Friend, children of
Gadget
Garage
Gather the facts
General trade
Gossip
Gossiper
Hands and arms
Happenstance
Home, mobile
Idea
Information
Inquiry
Instruction
Intellectual activity
Investigation
Journalist
Journey

Journey partner
Juvenile
Kin
Kindred
Language
Lease as document
Lecturer
Lecturing
Letter
Letter
Librarian
Library
License, document
Linguist
Linguistic ability
Link
Literary ability
Literary work
Literature
Local matter
Lung
Magazine
Mail
Mailing
Manuscript as written document
Mass transit
Media
Meeting hall
Meeting, small gathering
Mental activity
Mental pursuit
Message
Messengers in general
Mind, the concrete
Mother, illness of
Motion
Motorcycle
Movement or travel, routine
Narrator
Near neighborhood
Near relative
Neighbor, dealing with
Neighbor
Neighborhood

*Astrological Keywords*

Neighborhood interest
Neighboring environment
Nervous system and illness
Networking
News, receiving
News, those who bring
News
Newspaper
Notary
Note
Papers
Perceiving
Perception
Periodical
Phone call
Phone
Post office
Postal system
Postal worker
Press
Printer
Printing
Private studies
 Publication, ephemeral
Publicity, personal
Pupil
Question
Radio as communication
Railroad
Reason
Reasoning ability
Relative
Reporter
Respiration
Road
Rumors and lies
Sales promotion
Salesperson
Scholar
School, elementary
School
Schooling
Schoolmate
Selling
Short trip
Shoulder
Sibling, dealing with
Sibling
Sign a contract

Signing of papers
Sister
Sorrel
Speaker
Speaking
Speech
Stenographer
Storm, effects of
Street
Student
Studies
Taking for granted, background
Talk
Talkers
Talking
Tape recorder
Teacher
Teaching
Telegraph
Telephone
Telephone system
Test, written or oral
Thoughts
Tie of consanguinity
Tongue
Tourist
Tradespeople
Traffic
Train
Transit
Transport
Transportation
Travel, local
Travel agent
Traveler
Trip
Trotting
Trudging
Typewriter
Typist
Utilities
Vehicle
Ventilation
Visit
Visitor
Voice
Window
Witness statement
Words

Writer
Writing skills
Writings
Written document

# Fourth House

Accommodations
Affairs of parents
Affairs of late life
Agricultural product
Agriculture
Ancestor
Ancient dwelling
Antique
Anything hidden in the ground
Apartment
Arena of action in the contest
Base of operations
Basement
Basic security
Beach
Beneath the ground
Boardinghouse
Breast
Builder
Building
Burial
Cafeteria
Career of partner
Castle
Cattle rancher
Cemetery
Cemetery plot
Child, conception of
City
Clan
Community affairs
Community
Community experience of weather
Conditions at close of life
Consequence, remote
Court decision in criminal case
Court decision in arbitration
Cousin, maternal
Crop
Damage from natural disaster
Damage from earthquake
Decision of a court
Demise
Digestive organ
Disaster, natural
Domestic interest
Domestic chore
Domestic affairs
Dormitory
Dwelling
Ecology
Elder
Elderly, the
Emotional security
Emotional need
End of long-term affairs
End of existence
End of the matter
End-of-life
Ending
Estate (land, real estate)
Experience
Factory
Family
Family affairs
Farm
Farmer
Father
Feeling of security
Field
Final outcome of any question
Final resort
Final resting place
Food, place where kept
Fortification
Foundation of building
Foundation in general
Friend's health
Furniture
Gallery
Garden
Gardener
Grave
Gravedigger
Ground, the
Hazard from natural phenomena
Hereditary trait
Hidden thing
Hidden matters
History
Home life, early
Home, quality of
Home, mobile
Home life
Home
Home environment
Hotel
House one purchases if one doesn't own a house
House
House one lives in or owns
House for sale
Housing
In the moment
Inheritance by descent
Instincts
Juror
Jury
Kitchen
Land
Large tree
Last illness
Later life
Lawn
Lawsuit, defendant in
Lawsuit, results of
Mine
Miner
Mineral product
Mining
Mislaid item
Money, recovery of loss
Monument
Motherhood
Museum
Natural resources
Nature of the ground purchased
North
Office or base of operations
Office where one works
Old age
Orchard

Astrological Keywords

Outcome of the matter, final
Outcome
Pantry
Parent-in-law
Parks and preserves (gardens)
Pasture
People, common
Place where business is conducted
Place of residence
Political party not in power
Present residence
Privacy
Produce and agricultural interests
Property matters
Property damage
Property damage from flood or earthquake
Quality of land or house
Rain
Rancher
Real estate, purchasing
Real estate, quality of
Real estate
Real estate transaction
Recovered wealth
Redecorating the home
Relations with parent
Relations with family
Remodeling
Residence
Restaurant
Result of a lawsuit
Roots
Safety
Secret belief
Security
Stomach
Superstition
Swimming pool
Tenement
Thief, hiding place of
Those residing in one's home
Those residing in querent's house
Thrill of the ride
Tillage of the earth
Tomb
Towns
Treasure hidden or buried
Under the earth

Underhandedness
Village
Warehouse
Wealth, recovered
Weather
Well
Where living things grow
Womb
Yard

# Fifth House

Abortion, spontaneous
Acting
Actor
Adornment
Adultery
Affairs of the heart
Affection
Ale house
Ambassador
Ammunition of a besieged town
Amusement park
Amusements
Animal
Anyone who is a stranger
Artistic output
Athletic contest
Athletic sports for show or gain
Aunt, illness
Avocation
Awareness
Baby
Baby shower
Back, upper
Back, anatomy
Bar (tavern)
Bedroom
Beloved pet
Bets and betting
Bingo
Birth rate
Boat
Cards, playing
Celebration as festival
Ceremony
Chance
Chance, operation of the law of
Chance, things that depend on
Child, dealing with
Child
Child, biological
Child, legitimacy of
Child, conception of
Child's affairs
Child's brain
Childbirth
Cinema as entertainment
Clothing as vanity
Cocktail party
Color, white
Color, honey
Community property
Community resources
Competition
Concert
Courtship
Creative activity
Creative talent
Creative work
Creative writing
Creativity
Dance
Dating
Death of a career
Death of a parent
Decorations
Delight
Dining out
Dinner engagement
Diplomat from foreign country
Display or ostentation
Dissipation
Education
Education, junior high
Educational pursuit
Educational matters
Effort to promote self
Election
Emotional expression
Emotional desires
Emotions, pleasurable
Enjoyment
Entertainer
Entertainment
Estate of the father
Examination
Excess
Exhibitionism
Expression
Favorite activity
Fertility
Festival
Film actor
Financial speculation
Fireplace
Flings and love affairs
Flirtation
Foolhardiness
Freedom, concept of
Freedom
Fun house
Fun
Gambling, lottery and gaming wheels
Game
Game of chance
Gender of the fetus
Giving love
Government representative
Grandiosity
Gratification
Hazard
Heart condition
Heart
High society
High, getting
Hobby
Hobby, creative
Holiday, vacation
Honeymoon
Horse racing
Indulgence
Innkeeper
Investigation
Jewelry
Jewelry as adornment or vanity
Jockey
Leadership
Learning, process of
Leisure activity
Liberty, personal
Literary creative output
Liver

Living
Loss of public office
Lost possession
Love of pleasure
Love questions
Love affairs
Loved one, dealing with
Lovers
Luck
Lying
Making love
Mansions and estates, great
Masturbation
Matters of the heart
Merriment
Messenger in general
Messenger of a republic
Messenger as personal ambassador
Miscarriage
Money of a parent
Motion picture industry
Musician
Narcissism
Night town
Object of affection
Offspring, physical or mental
Opera
Ornament
Ostentatious behavior
Ownership
Palace
Parade
Parent, death of
Parks and recreation
Party
Passion
Personal creativity
Pet as surrogate child
Petition
Picnic
Place of water or plumbing
Place of amusement
Play
Play, for fun
Playground
Pleasant time
Pleasurable pursuit
Pleasure
Political election

Pomp and circumstance
Power of attorney
Pregnancy, state of a woman with child
Pregnancy and child birth
Pride
Procreation
Project of the querent
Promoter
Proxy
Public school system
Racetrack
Radio and entertainment
Raffle
Real estate, income from
Recklessness
Recreation
Recreational sex
Relaxation
Representation of self
Resort area
Resort
Rock concert
Romance without commitment
Romance
School, secondary
School function
Seeking of admiration
Self-centeredness
Self-expression
Self-wastage
Sex, recreational
Sex object
Sex
Sexual activity
Sexual intercourse
Sexual pleasure
Social function
Social affair
Sorrow, public
Soul
Speculation
Speculative stocks and bonds
Sporting event
Sports
Stock exchange
Stock market
Stockholder
Stomach

Sweetheart
Take chances
Tavern
Teacher
Teaching
Theater
Uncle, illness of
Uncle, paternal
Upper class
Upper legislative house
Vacation
Vanity
Wardrobe
Warmest part of the house
Wedding announcement
Will of the father
Young people, dealing with

# Sixth House

Abdomen
Abrasion
Accountant
Action that affects health
Agency
Agent
Air conditioning
Allergy
Animal husbandry
Animal, small domesticated
Antibiotic
Appliance
Apprenticeship
Archivist
Armed services
Army
Artificial limb
Aunt
Aunt, paternal
Aunts and uncles, generic
Bird as pet
Boarders and tenants
Bodily well being
Book
Bookkeeper
Bowels
Bus person
Butler
Cafeteria
Care of pet
Careful
Caretaker
Care for others
Categorization
Celibacy
Chemist
Civil service
Civil service worker
Client
Climate
Clinic
Clothing in general
Clothing, useful
Comforts like food and clothing
Commodities
Computer programmer
Conservation
Conserving
Container
Cooking
Coworker
Crafts
Craftsmanship
Credit union
Critic
Crop
Daily duties
Day laborer
Deference
Deliberation of a jury
Dentist and dentistry
Dependent
Details and detailing
Diet
Dietary habit
Dietitian
Disagreeable duty
Discipleship
Discrimination
Disease
Distress and distressing conditions
Dog
Domestic chore
Domestic servant
Drawer
Drudgery
Druggist
Drugs
Drugstore clerk
Drycleaner
Duties, daily
Eating habits
Efficiency
Efficient routine
Employee
Employment
Employment matters
Everyday activities
Eyeglasses
False teeth
Farmer
Father's kin
Fatigue
File cabinet
Food
Food industry
Food market
Food preparation
Food service
Food, where kept
Food, where dispersed
Frustrations that cause illness
Furniture
Gauge
Goat
Grain
Grocery store
Habit, personal
Handicrafts
Hard work
Hare
Healer
Healing
Health
Health food
Health improvement program
Health, poor
Health, problem with
Hearing aid
Hiring of employee
Hog
Home of a sibling
Home of a neighbor
House servant
Husbandry
Hygiene
Hypochondriac
Illness
Income property
Indigestion
Inferior
Inferior part of the belly

Astrological Keywords

Infirmary
Infirmity
Inoculation
Insurance, unemployment
Intestine
Item for practical comfort
Job, seeking if one has a job
Job, work at
Job opportunity
Jury deliberation
Labor force
Labor
Labor trouble
Labor strike
Labor union
Laborer
Laboring class
Leader
Legal office
Librarian
Livestock company
Lodger
Magic performed by querent
Maid
Mail carrier
Maladjustments in general
Marketing
Masseur
Measuring device
Medical office
Medicine
Mental strain
Mental health worker
Microscope
Military service
Military
Mother, journey of
Navy
Necessity of life
Nervous aggravation
Nurse
Nursing
Nutrition
Occupation
Office of an agent
Office where one works
Organized labor
Overly tired
Overstrained

Paternal, kindred
Peptic ulcer
Personnel
Pet
Pharmacy
Physical examination
Physical discomfort
Physician
Place where records are stored
Pocket
Police, as civil servant
Precision
Preserving
Preventative medicine
Proactive
Psychiatric treatment
Psychiatrist
Public works
Public health
Public servant
Rabbit
Real estate agent
Record keeper
Recovery of sick person
Rectum
Regimentation
Regrets
Relationship, unusual
Renter
Repair work
Restaurant
Salvaging
Sanitation
Secretary
Selvage
Servant
Servants of the country
Serve, capacity to
Service, necessary
Service repair person
Service, people who give
Service, being of
Service of repair peerson
Service
Service to others
Service rendered or received
Service, volunteer
Serving
Servitude

Sewing
Sheep
Shepherd
Shop
Sickness quality and cause
Sickroom
Side, wound to
Skin conditions
Slave
Social Security
Solar plexus
Stenographer
Steward
Stored product
Storehouse for dairy products
Storehouse
Stress
Strike, inception
Strike, labor
Studios
Submission
Subordinate
Subordinate role
Subservience
Surgical supplies
Tenants and lodgers
Therapeutic activity
Thermostat
Those who tend to the sick
Those who deal with clothing
Tool
Towel
Trade union
Trades people
Treatment, medical
Tuberculosis
Typist
Uncle
Unemployment insurance
Uniform
Veterinarian
Vitamin
Waiter
Waitress
Watchman
Weather
Work with heavy tools
Work
Work area

Work habit
Work room
Work schedule
Work environment
Work conditions
Worker in any trade
Worker
Worker at a routine job for wages
Working class
Workmen's Compensation
Workshop
X-ray operator
Zoo

# Seventh House

Adversary
Advisor, personal
Agent of the querent
Agreement
Alliance
Ally
Anyone unrelated by blood
Arbitrator
Argument
Arts, fine arts
Associate
Astrological counselor
Athletic contest
Back, lower
Balance
Banished person
Battle
Beauty, things of
Bonding with others
Burglar
Business
Business associate
Business partnership
Buttocks
Buyer
Challenger in a contest
Change of locale
Claw
Cohabitation prompted by love
Combat
Commitment
Competition
Competitor
Compromise
Consultant, personal
Consultation from an expert
Contact with equals
Contest
Contestant
Contested matter
Contract, legal or social
Contract between partners
Contractual agreement
Controversy
Convict, escaped
Cooperation with others
Cooperative arrangement
Counselor
Court decision in arbitration
Covenant
Criminal on trial
Criminal at large
Customer
Deal
Defendant in lawsuit
Dispute
Dissolution of partnership
Divorce
Doctor to querent
Duel
Education, high school
Enemy, open
Escaped convict
Expelled party
Fine arts
Friend, close
Fugitive
General public
Grandfather (paternal)
Grandmother (maternal)
Grandparents
House one plans to move to
I.O.U.
Immediate outcome of event
Joint activity
Joint venture
Kidney
Lawbreaker
Lawsuit, result of
Lawsuit
Lawyer of querent in a court action
Lease as agreement
Legal contract
Legal dispute
Legal action
Living room
Love question
Marriage, proposed
Marriage, separation in
Marriage and other unions
Mate
Meditation
Money from renter or tenant
Money from person from whom
    one borrows
Move, propose place to move to
Murder victim
Murderer
Naval
Nephew
New place of residence
Niece
Nieces and nephews
Office of the partner
Open adversary
Open warfare
Opposite party
Organ donor
Organized crime
Other party in a contest
Other side in a issue
Other place
Other people
Outcome of contentions
Outcome of opposition
Outcome of the matter, immediate
Outlawed person
Ovary
Paramour
Partner
Partner's room
Partnership
Party to a contract
People, common
People, other people in general
Person, missing
Person stealing
Person inquired about
Physician
Physician as querent's advisor
Place where partner spends most of
    the time

Astrological Keywords

Place where people gather
Power of attorney
Prisoner, escaped
Prize fight
Public relations
Public negotiations
Public enemy
Public gathering
Quarrel
Reciprocal arrangements
Relations with the public
Relationship, interpersonal
Relationship, committed
Relationship, equal
Relationship, contractual
Rent from a tenant
Response
Responsible
Rival
Robber
Romance with commitment
Runaway
School, secondary
Seller
Separation
Settlement of dispute
Sharing
Shopper
Sponsor
Spouse
Stolen thing
Stranger
Street
Sweethearts
Teammate
Teamwork
Theft
Thief
Those who meet in public
Those one consults
Treaty
Trial
Undesignated other person
Union of two people
Union
Urge to adapt to others
Verdict of the jury
Victor in battle
War

Warlike situation
West
Where one wishes to relocate
Wife
Yoga
Yoke

A.I.D.S.

# Eighth House

Abortion, surgical
Abrasion
Abuse
Accountant
Alchemy
Alimony
Alteration
Analysis
Astral experience
Audit, tax or financial
Bail bond
Bankruptcy
Bare bones
Bathroom
Bedroom
Beginning, new
Bill
Birth
Birth control
Bladder
Bowel movement
Bribery
Brothel
Brutality
Business
Butcher
Cadaver
Cemetery
Cesspool
Change
Charge card
Charge account
Cleaning out
Clearing away
Community property
Compelling force
Compulsion
Compulsive sex
Coroner
Corporation, restructuring of
Corpse
Cosmetic surgery
Credit union
Credit, financial

Crematory
Crime
Criticism
Cut
Damage
Danger
Death
Death, cause of
Death, loss and gain because of
Death, manner of
Death of someone inquired about
Death, physical and spiritual
Debt
Debt, recovery of
Decay
Demise
Destroyer
Destruction
Detective
Disaster, natural
Disease, sexually transmitted
Disembodied entity
Donation
Dowry
Dump
Elimination
Emotions, intense
Epidemic
Escrow on property
Escrow account
Exchange
Excretion
Executioner
Exhaust system
External sex organ
Extreme
Famine
Fateful loss
Fears and worries
Feces
Fee
Finances of spouse
Financial condition of partnership
Financial settlement

Financial advisor
Financial relations with competitor
Financial obligations of querent
Fine
Gambling, insolvency from
Garbage disposal
Garbage can
Genitals
Gifts and legacies one receives
Grant
Gratuity
Hair transplant
Healer
Healing
Healing crisis
Hemorrhoid
Hidden matter
Hidden talent
Incest
Income tax return
Income from others
Inheritance
Inhibiting factor
Injury
Insect
Installment buying
Insurance
Insurance, unemployment
Insurance policy
Insurance, life
Insurance settlement
Interest rate
Investigator
Jealousy
Joint savings
Joint finances
Junk
Kidney stone
Killing
Laboratory
Last will and testament
Laundry room
Lending agency
Liability, financial

Astrological Keywords

Libido
Lien
Loan
Loss in general
Main bathroom
Malice
Manipulation of another
Martial arts
Masturbation
Medicaid
Medical discovery
Mind, anguish
Mind, unconscious
Monetary partnership
Money the querent owes another
Money, place where kept
Money of the dead
Money, the public's
Money of others
Money and possessions of a partner
Money, inherited
Money for retirement
Money by marriage
Mortality
Mortgage
Mortgage company
Motive, inner
Murder victim
Muscular system
Obsession
Occult matters
Occult experience
Pallbearer
Partnership finances
Penetration
Peril
Plague
Poison
Pollution
Private parts
Probate
Probe
Profit of a partnership
Profit from move
Property escrow
Property tax
Prostitute
Prostitution
Psychoanalyst

Psychological counseling
Psychologist
Psychology, deep
Purification
Rebirth
Recovery of debt
Reduction
Reform
Refuse
Regeneration
Rejuvenation
Renewal
Renovation
Reorganization
Research
Researcher
Researching new methods
Restructuring a corporation
Retirement funds
Retirement income
Revision
Rodent
Rubbish
Sadness
Salvage
Sanitation
Savings
Séance room
Séance
Secret dealings
Secret
Septic tank
Settlement, financial
Sewer
Sex
Sex, orgasmic
Sex organ
Sexual activity
Sexual intercourse
Sexual release
Sexual power
Sexual energy
Sexual disease
Sexual merging
Sexuality
Shared expense
Shared asset
Shrewdness
Social Security

Spiritual rebirth
Stab
Surgeon
Surgery
Suspicion
Tariff
Tax consultant
Tax audit
Tax collector
Tax, income tax return
Taxes
Therapeutic activity
Tip
Title to property
Title search
Toxic waste
Transformation
Transition
Trust fund
Undertaker
Unwilling conformity
Upheaval
Urination
Venereal disease
Victim of a murder
Violent crime
Waste and those who waste
Wills and legacies
Workmen's Compensation
Wound




















Abstract thinking

# Ninth House

Abstraction
Academia
Academic aims
Academic subject
Accident, liability of
Advanced degree
Advertising department
Advertising
Affairs of in-laws
Agent of justice
Airplanes
Airport
Alien
Altruism
Altruistic undertaking
Analysis
Astrology
Attic
Attitude toward God
Attorney
Bare bones
Belief system
Bird, in flight
Bishop
Book
Border, across the
Brother-in-law
Business dealings abroad
Ceremony that legalizes a matter
Ceremony as an official character
Chapel
Church
Church matters
Clergy
Code of ethics
College
Color, white
Comet
Communication, long distance
Conceptual framework
Conferences, large meeting
Convocation
Corporation
Court of law
Court procedure
Court of justice
Court case
Creative manipulation of idea
Crossing the border
Cultural knowledge
Culture
Detonation
Diploma
Disciplined thought
Dissemination of knowledge
Distance, things at a
Distant shores
Distant connection
Distant relative
Distant place
Distant contacts and interests
Disturbance, origin of
Divination
Divorce proceeding
Dream as a mental journey
Dreams and visions
Education, specialized
Education, adult class
Education, higher
Education
Education, religious
Educational institution, relationship with
Educator
Essentials
Ethical responsibility
Ethics
Examination
Exotic land
Expansion
Explorer
Export
Extension
Faith
Far neighborhood
Flying saucer
Forecasting
Foreign country
Foreign item
Foreigner
Freedom
Friend of a friend
Future, foreseeing
Future plans
Generalization
Going abroad
Graduation
Grandchildren
Guru
Hazard from natural phenomena
Healing after an operation
Higher studies
Hip
Import and exports
Import-export business
In-law
Inauguration
Indemnity for damage suffered
Inheritance
Inspiration
Insurance company
Insurance for fire and damage
Insurance
Insurance adjuster
Insurance, compensation from
Insurance agent
Intellectual pursuit
Interstate commerce
Intuition
Jesuit
Journey to a distant place
Judge
Jurisprudence
Jury duty
Justice
Kindred of the spouse
Knowledge
Language, foreign
Large
Law
Lawyers, as a class
Learning, advanced

*Astrological Keywords*

Learning, higher
Lecturer
Lecturing
Legal action
Legal activity
Legal advice
Legal affairs
Legal claim
Legal, make something
Legal practices
Legal procedures and transactions
Legal question
Legalization, process of
Legalize by ceremony or ritual
Liability to accident
Literature
Long journey
Long-range plans
Lucky break
Marketing
Marriage vow
Meeting
Meeting, large gathering
Metaphysics
Mind, the abstract
Mind, developments of the
Mind, super conscious
Minister, clergyperson
Monk
Morals
Navy
Neighbor of spouse
Office of an agent
Origin of disturbance
Orthodox religions
Orthodox observations
Outcome of illness
Overseas
Parade
People at a distance
Person, absent
Person, missing
Person, religious
Philosopher
Philosophic society
Philosophy
Physician
Pilot
Place that is high

Plan ahead
Political propaganda
Prayer
Preacher
Priest
Probate
Professional
Professional class
Professor
Proficiency in a science
Prognostication
Propaganda
Prophecy
Prophet
Prophetic dream
Prophetic vision
Protection
Public convention
Public meeting
Public opinion
Public relations
Publication, non-ephemeral
Publicity
Publicity director
Publisher
Publishing
Purification
Rabbi
Radio broadcasting
Reason
Refugee
Religion
Religious preferment
Religious worker
Religious affairs
Religious education
Remote place
Retirement funds
Rituals
Satellite
Scholar
Science
Science of astrology
Scientific society
Scientist
Sea voyage
Shrine
Significant visions
Sky, things in the

Social Security
Spirit
Spirituality
Sports
Spouse's sibling
Storm, incoming (process of formation)
Stranger
Subpoena
Success in law, science, religion
Supreme Court
Surgery, healing
Systematic thinking
Teacher
Teaching
Theoretical direction of research
Thigh
Those in an artistic career
Those in a ceremony
Those of a different background
Those of a different race
Those of wealth and influence
Those dealing with future trends
Transportation over long distance
Travel agent
Travel by air
Travel, long distance
Traveler, world
Traveler
Trip
Trip of partner, short
Truth
University
Upper level
Vagrant
Visions
Voyage
Weather conditions along the coast
Weather forecaster
Wedding
What lasts
Wider vision
Winnings
Wisdom
World view
World assembly (e.g., U.N.)
Worldwide contacts

Achievement

# Tenth House

Active head of an enterprise
Administration
Administrator
Advancement
Affairs of official
Affairs of parent
Ambition
Arbitrator
Aristocracy
Attainment
Auction
Authority and authority figures
Awakening
Award
Bone
Boss
Business
Business or professional standing
Business world
Business, place of
Business affairs
Business, big
Business success
Career activities
Career
Chairman of the board
Chief executive
City official
Clairvoyance
Color, white
Commander-in-chief
Concrete structure
Conviction and execution in trial
Corporation asset
Court
Court in questions of law
Cousin
Cousin, paternal
Credit as reputation
Credit
Department store
Dictator
Dignitary
Dignity
Dining room
Discipline, those who enforce it
Duke
Dukedom
Earl
Emperor
Employer
Employment
Executive work
Executive
Executive head of an enterprise
Fall from power
Fame
Famous person
Fate
Father-in-law
Foreman
Gain from long journey
Gains through science
Glory
Governing authority
Government, dealing with
Government agency
Government official
Government, head of
Government
Government, affairs of
Governor
Guardian
Hallway
Head of an organization
Higher-up
Honor
Honors
House, price of
Infamy
Influential person
Judge
Judge, decision in a lawsuit
Jury as an executive body
Justice of the peace
King
Knee
Land, price of
Land developer
Landlord
Landowner
Law
Law enforcement
Leader
Litter, animal
Management
Manager
Marriage, end of
Master
Mayor
Monarch
Mother
Notoriety
Occupation (as opposed to job)
Office, gaining an
Office, status
Office of the partner
Officer in authority
Official
Official business
Organization
Out-of-body
Oversight
People, forcible control of
People, powerful
People in power
People, eminent
People, important
Person of rank
Person having authority over querent
Person holding office
Person, great
Personal affairs
Picture, big
Political preferment
Political party in power
Political success
Popularity
Position in society
Power to achieve worldly success
Power

*Astrological Keywords*

Practical insight
Practical talent
Preferment
President
Prestige
Prime minister
Princess
Profession
Professional
Profit of publication
Profit from a corporation
Promotion
Public recognition
Public status
Public office
Public's attention
Publicity
Rank
Real estate of spouse
Realization of ambition
Realization
Recognition
Referee in a contest
Relationship with those in authority
Reputation
Responsibility
Ruler
Shop of the querent
Social recognition
Social place or standing
South
Status
Structure
Success
Success in politics
Superior, contact with
Superior
Those in authority
Those in responsible positions
Those noticed by the public
Victory
Vocation
Worldly position

Acquaintance, new

# Eleventh House

Acquaintance
Advisor
Affiliation in groups
Alderman
Altruism
Altruistic undertaking
Ankle
Associate
Astrological affairs
Board of directors
Business income
Business asset
Career, money from
Cause
Celebration as festival
Ceremony as group function
Chamber of commerce
Child, adopted
Child of another
Child, step
Child-in-law
Circumstances beyond querent's control
Circumstantial development
City council
Club
Club member
Color, yellow
Color, saffron
Commodity exchange
Community of fraternal groups
Community affairs
Community
Confidence
Congress
Counselor
Coworker
Criticism, friendly
Daughter-in-law
Dearest wish
Death in the family
Death of parent
Desires
Eccentric
Electrician
Emotional desires
Employer's financial condition
Flatterer
Foster child
Fraternal groups and organizations
Friend
Friendly help
Friends, get-togethers with
Friendship
Friendship, ties of
Future plans
Gadget
Ghost
Goal
Group activity
Group, ties with
Group work
Group interest
Group connection
Group gathering
Group, fraternal
Happenstance
Happiness, idea of
Hopes and wishes
Hotel stay at a distance
House of Representatives
Humanitarian activities and ideas
Idea, new
Illness of pet
Income from business or career
Independence
Intentions
Job one seeks while already employed
Jury as a counseling body
Lecture
Leg from the knee to the ankle
Legislation
Legislative activities and bodies
Legislator
Lodge, fraternal
Love, receiving
Lower legislative house
Marriage of a child
Marriage, discord or happiness in
Marriage, happiness of
Meeting hall
Membership
Mob
Modern gadget
Money of a business
Money from career
Money of parent
Money, parent's
Money, mother's
New age gadget
Nonconformist
Objectives in general
Organization
Parent, death of
Parliament
People, other
People, eccentric
Pilot
Praise
Profit of a business
Psychiatrist
Psychological counseling
Rebel
Receiving love
Regulation
Relationship, unbonded
Relationship, foster
Relationship, platonic
Residence while abroad
Salary
Scientist
Senate
Senator
Social affair
Social alliance
Social contact
Social life
Social tie
Society
Son-in-law
State legislature

*Astrological Keywords*

Step-child
Stock exchange
Surprise
Thinker, free
Town council
Treasury
Trust
Usual method
Vicarious experience
Wages
Well wisher
What should be
Women's liberation
X-ray

Acceptance

# Twelfth House

Addict
Advanced degree
Affliction
Alcoholism
Ambush
Animal in a zoo
Animal, large or wild
Animal beyond control
Animals, threatening
Ashram
Assassin
Assassination
Asylum
Aunt
Bad habit
Bail, get out on
Banished person
Beggar
Behind the scenes
Bird, wild
Blackmail
Blasphemy
Bondage
Bribery
Burglar
Burglary
Captivity
Car, used car salesperson
Cattle, large
Character defect
Charitable act
Charitable institution
Charity given and received
Charity
Child, death of
Chronic illness
Clairvoyance
Clandestine affairs
Clandestine associate
Clandestine work
Clinic
Compassion
Concentration camp
Concern for others
Confidence
Confidential matters
Confidential affairs
Confidential agent
Confinement, any type
Conspiracy
Contact with an invalid
Contrition
Convent
Convention, large meeting
Convict, escaped
Correctional institution
Courtroom
Crime
Criminal
Crying
Daydreaming
Deception
Defeat
Defects of character
Delusion
Detective
Detention
Disappointment
Displaced person
Doctor's office
Doom
Dream and sleep patterns
Drug
Drug addiction
Drug dealer
Drug, illicit
Drunkard
Dues
Education, specialized
Elephant
Emotional problem
Endings
Enemies, secret
Enemies, in general
Epidemic
Error in judgment
Escape from bondage
Escaped convict
Escapism
Estrangement
Failure
Fears and worries
Feet
Film
Food stamp
Forces inclined to dissolution
Foreign spy
Forgetfulness
Fraud
Freedom
Frustrations
Frustrations that cause illness
Funeral
Gambling, illicit
Game preserve
Ghetto
Ghost
Ghost town
Grief
Guard
Hallucination
Handicap
Hangover
Hemmed in
Hidden defect
Hidden factors
Hidden fears
Hidden matters
Hidden problem
Hidden vice
Hindering factor
Home for the aged
Homeless people
Horse
Hospital
Hospitalization
House of detention
Hypnotist
Illness, incurable
Illness of partner
Illusion
Impractical idea

Astrological Keywords

Imprisonment
Inadequacy of self
Infirmary
Informer
Inhibiting factor
Inhibition
Inner development
Institution
Institution
Institutionalization
Introspection
Invalid, contact with
Investigation
Investigative activity
Investigator
Involuntary service ordered by law
Involuntary incarceration
Jail
Jailer
Karma
Kidnap
Kidnapper
Kidnapping
Labor trouble
Labor strike
Labor union
Large animal
Large institution
Lessons learned
Liar
Library
Limiting conditions
Loneliness
Long-range plans
Loose ends
Magic performed by another
Maladjustment, psychological
Malice
Malicious person
Martyrdom
Maternal kindred
Medicaid
Medicine
Meditation
Mental health worker
Mental illness
Mind, unconscious
Mind, subconscious
Mindedness, absent

Mischief
Misery
Misfortune
Misfortune, unexpected
Misinformation
Monastery
Monk
Mother's kin
Mourning
Mysterious condition
Mysticism
Narcotic
Nervous breakdown
Nun
Nursing home
Obstacle
Occult matters
Occult society
Occupation involving unreality
Opposition, underhanded or sneaky
Opposition, behind the scenes
Organized crime activity
Organized crime
Orphan
Oxen
Panda bear
Pardon
Parole
Past mistake
Past, the
Past
Patience
Penitentiary
People, forcible control of
People, sleazy
Persecution
Persecutor
Personal limitations
Pharmacy
Philanthropic institution
Philosopher
Pipe dream
Place hidden or out of sight
Plague
Plots and schemes
Poison
Poverty
Prison

Prisoner, escaped
Privacy
Private problem
Private investigation
Private scandal
Private enemy
Private matters
Problem, personal
Prostitution, organized
Protective custody
Psychiatric treatment
Psychic influences
Psychic phenomena
Psychic
Psychic ability
Public institution
Punishment
Put up with
Quietude
Recluse
Reform school
Relationship, clandestine
Relationship, hidden
Relief work
Remote place
Renunciation
Repression
Reprieve
Research project
Research
Restraint
Restructuring condition
Retreat
Sacrifice
Sadness
Sea
Séance
Secluded place
Seclusion
Secret sorrows
Secret fears
Secret
Secret enemy
Secret organization
Secret society
Secret dealings
Secret Service
Self-analysis
Self-destruction

Self-injury
Self-sacrifice
Self-undoing
Self-wastage
Selfless giving
Service, selfless
Service freely given
Serving mankind
Shame
Sickroom
Sins of omission and commission
Skeleton in the closet
Slave
Sleep
Sneak
Solitary pursuit
Solitude
Sorrows
Spiritual matters
Spouse's health
Spy
Strike, labor
Subversion
Suffering
Suffering, silent
Suicide
Sympathy
Terrorist
Those who tend to the sick
Those under detention
Those on welfare
Time to be alone
Torment
Trade union
Tragedy
Treason
Tribulation
Turmoil, inner or psychic
Ulterior motive
Uncle, maternal
Undisclosed condition
Undoing
Unfortunates
University
Unreality
Unseen
Veterinarian
Welfare agency
Welfare worker

Welfare
Welfare recipient
Widow
Widowhood
Wilderness
Witchcraft
Withdrawal into fantasy
Work behind the scenes
Work done quietly or alone
Worries
Yesterday
Zoo

# Keywords for Planets

# Sun

Achievement
Acting
Active head of an enterprise
Acute fever
Administration
Administrator
Adornment
Advancement
Advertising
Amber stone
Ambition
Amusement
Amusement park
Angelica herb
Arrogance
Artery
Athletic sports for show or gain
Atom
Attainment
Authority and authority figure
Authority
Back, upper
Back, anatomy
Boasting
Boss
Carbuncle stone
Cardiac status
Cataract
Celebration as festival
Chakra, fourth, green
Chamomile herb
Chief executive
Cinnamon
Circulatory system
Citrus tree
Color, yellow
Color, saffron
Color, sandy
Color, orange
Commander
Competition
Conceit
Consciousness
Contest
Contestant
Creative energy
Creative talent
Creative writing
Creativity
Credit
Dandelion herb
Dating
Dawn
Daylight
Diamond stone
Dignitary
Dignity
Dining room
Display or ostentation
Drama
Egotism
Emperor
Employer
Energy
Entertainer
Entertainment
Executive work
Executive
Exhibitionism
Eye problem
Eye, left of female
Eye, right of male
Eyebright herb
Fame
Fame, giver of
Famous person
Father
Fever, dangerously high
Fever
Firefly
Fireplace
Foreman
Frankincense
Freedom
Fun
Gambling
Game
General well-being
Generosity
Glaucoma
Glory
Gold metal
Goldsmith
Governing authority
Government official
Government, head of
Government
Grandiosity
Grant
Guardian
Hall
Head of an organization
Health
Heart condition
Heart
Honey
Honors
Husband in a woman's chart
Husband
Identity, sense of
Influence
Influential person
Inner self
Integrity
Jewelry
Jockey
Juniper
Justice of the peace
King
Leader
Leadership
Life force
Lion
Liquor, rare
Lovage herb
Lover, male
Luck
Magistrate
Magnificent structure
Majesty
Male in authority
Male gender

Astrological Keywords

Manager
Managerial ability
Mansions and estates, great
Masculine principle
Men, ages 35 to 45
Men in general
Merriment
Midday
Monarch
Money, minter of
Myrrh
Narcissism
Nobility
Nobleman
Office holding
Official
Orange
Ornament
Ostentatious behavior
Palace
Peacock
People, important
People in power
People, haughty
Peppermint herb
Pimples on the face
Play for fun
Political preferment
Political election
Politician
Politics
Pomp and circumstance
Popularity
Position of power and authority
Position in society
Positions of management
Power
Preferment
Prestige
Pride
Prizefight
Promoter
Promotions
Public office
Public status
Public relations
Public attention
Publicity
Putting the best foot forward

Rank
Recklessness
Recognition
Recreation
Recuperation, powers of
Reddish complexion
Reforms
Regalia
Representation of the self
Reputation
Resort
Romance
Rosemary herb
Round object
Royalty and nobility
Ruler
Ruling class
Saffron herb
Seeking of admiration
Self-centeredness
Self-confidence
Self-expression
Self-wastage
Significance
Skylight
Spark of life
Spectacle as sight
Speculation
Spinal column
Spirit
Spleen
Sporting event
Sports
Status
Success
Sunday
Sunflower
Sunstroke
Superior
Superiority
Survival
Take chances
Theater
Things that are noticed
Those in authority
Those publicly noticed
Title
Tree, rare
Upper-class

Vacation
Vanity
Vehicle, magnificent
Warmest part of the house
Well-being
Wine, fine
Wood stove
Wood, rare
Worldly position

# Moon

Abscess
Accommodations
Agriculture
Alcoholism
Allergic substance
Ambassador
Animal, missing
Antique
Assimilation
Baby
Babysitter
Baker
Baptize
Basic security
Bathing
Beach
Beverage
Boat, small
Body fluids
Brain
Breast
Brewer
Brewing
Cabbage
Cafeteria
Canal
Cancer
Caretaker
Caterer
Cauliflower
Cemetery plot
Chakra, third, yellow
Change
Changeable condition
Cheese
Chef
Chicken
Child, conception of
Child, female
Childbirth
Chinaware
Clam
Cleaner
Closet
Collection
Color, aqua
Color, green
Color, pale yellowish white
Color, pale green
Color, silver
Color, white
Commerce
Commodity
Common touch
Concave or wavy object
Container
Cook
Cooking
Crops
Crowd of people
Crystals stone
Cucumber
Cupboard
Daily life
Dairy
Dealer in liquids
Depression
Desires
Digestion
Digestive organs
Dock
Domestic affairs
Domesticity
Drunkard
Duck
Electorate
Embryo
Emotional security
Emotional problems
Emotional needs
Emotionally inhibited
Emotions
Epilepsy
Evening
Eye, left male
Eye, right of female
Faint
Family
Family affairs
Feeling of security
Feelings
Feldspar
Female function
Female relations
Ferry worker
Fertility
Fickleness
Fisher
Fluctuation
Fluid balance of the body
Fluid retention
Food
Fugitive
Functioning
Gain publicity
General public
Gestation
Gland
Glandular secretion
Goose
Gout
Grocery
Growth
Habit pattern
Happenstance
Herb, mild
Historian
History
Home environment
Home
Homemaker
House servant
Household affairs
Housekeeper
Housing
Humor
Husbandry
Imagination
Impressionable
Inferiors
Inheritance by descent
Insanity

Astrological Keywords

Instincts
Jade stone
Janitor
Journey by water
Journey
Kitchen
Lake
Land
Laundress
Linen
Liquid
Lobster
Lost thing
Luncheon
Lymphatic system
Magnesium
Maid
Mariner
Mass of people
Matron
Measles
Melon
Member of a wedding
Memory
Menses
Menstruation
Messengers in general
Midwife
Milk delivery person
Miller
Mind, subconscious
Missing thing
Mistress
Monday
Mood
Moonstone stone
Mother
Motherhood
Mucous membrane
Mystery
Navigation
Navy
News
Non-distinction
Nourishment
Nurse
Nursery, baby
Nursing
Nutrition

Obesity
Obstetrics
Omen
Ordinary business
Otter
Ovary
Passivity
Pearl stone
People, common
Person, missing
Person, absent and not related to querent
Personality
Phase of the tides
Phase
Pilgrim
Plant
Plastic
Popularity
Pregnancy and childbirth
Protective urge
Psychic ability
Psychosomatic disease
Public
Public, dealings with
Pumpkin
Quiet
Rabbit
Rain
Receptivity
Reflex
Relations with the public
Resident
Response
Responsiveness
Restaurant
Romance, idealistic Notoriety
Runaway
Sailing
Sailor
Saxifrage herb
Sciatica
Sea, product of the
Seashore
Security
Servant
Shopkeeper
Shyness
Small boat

Sot
Stolen thing
Stomach
Stray animal
Superstition
Swimming pool
Swimming
Tarragon herb
Tavern
Tear duct
Temporary plan
Those who work with liquids
Tide
Travel, local
Traveler
Trip
Trivial matter
Tumor
Turtle
Upsetting conditions
Urge for security
Uterus
Vacillation
Vagabond
Verbena herb
Voter
Voyage
Wanderlust
Washing machine
Water
Where living things grow
White milk
Wife
Woman inquired about
Womb
Women in general
Women
Work with liquids
Youngster

# Mercury

Abdomen
Ability as agent/speaker/teacher
Accident
Accuracy
Ad writer
Adaptability
Advertisement, written copy
Advertiser
Agate stone
Agency
Agent
Agreement, written document
Ambassador
Analysis
Analytical scientist
Aniseed herb
Annoyance
Anonymous letter
Ant
Aquamarine stone
Architect
Arm
Armed services
Art supplies
Asthma
Author
Automobile
Awareness
Balm herb
Bee
Bird, talking
Bird, carrier pigeon
Book
Bookkeeper
Bookkeeping
Bookworm
Bowels
Box
Brain
Breathing
Brokerage
Bronchitis
Brother
Bus
Bus driver
Business person
Busybody
Cafeteria
Calamint
Camera
Car
Car repair
Caraway herb
Caraway, seed
Carrot
Cat
Categorization
Check
Child, young
Civil engineer
Clerical worker
Clerk
Clerking
Cleverness
Client
Close relative
Clothing in general
Color, checked
Color, azure blue
Color, slate
Comings and goings
Commodity
Communication, skill at
Communication
Commuter
Commuting
Computer
Computer technician
Conference, large meeting
Container
Contract, signing of
Contract, written document
Conversation
Conveyance
Correspondence
Cousin, generic
Coworker
Craftsperson
Critic
Curiosity
Daily comings and goings
Dealer
Decision
Deed, written
Delirium
Delivery person
Delivery
Dependent
Desk
Details and detailing
Dexterity
Diet
Dietitian
Difference
Dill herb
Discrimination
Discussion
Dissemination of knowledge
Doctor
Document
Dog
Driving
Drudgery
Dry cough
Drycleaner
Duty, daily
Editing
Editor
Education, lower
Education
Efficiency
Efficient routine
Eloquence
Emotional capacity and technique
Employee
Everyday duty
Examination
Expression
Farmer
Fellow employee
Fickleness
File cabinet

Astrological Keywords

File
Finger
Food
Footman
Forger
Fox
Garage
Gathering of facts
Gauge
General trade
Giddiness
Gossip
Gossiper
Graphology
Grocery store
Guide
Ham radio
Hands and arms
Happenstance
Harmonica
Headache
Healer
Healing measure of any sort
Health food
Hiring of employee
Hoarseness
Hormone
House servant
Hypochondriac
Idea
Illness
Indigestion
Infirmary
Information
Ingenuity
Inquiry
Inquisitiveness
Insect, small and annoying
Instruction
Instrument, wind
Intellectual object
Intellectual pursuit
Intelligence
Intelligent
Interpretation
Intestine
Inventor
Irritation
Jewelry, costume

Journalist
Journey
Journey of a partner
Juvenile
Key
Kin
Labor
Language
Lavender herb
Learning
Lease as document
Lease as agreement
Lecturer
Lecturing
Legal contract
Letter
Librarian
Library
License document
Lilac flower
Linguist
Linguistic ability
Literary ability
Literary person
Literary work
Literature
Local matters
Logic
Loom
Luggage
Lung
Lung disease
Machinery operated by hand
Magazine
Maid
Mail
Mail carrier
Mailing
Manuscript as written document
Marjoram herb
Market
Marketing
Mathematician
Measuring device
Meddlesome
Media
Medicine
Meeting, small gathering
Memory problem

Memory
Mental activity
Mental pursuit
Mental strain
Merchandise
Merchandising
Merchant
Message
Messengers in general
Mind, the concrete
Mirror
Mob
Modern gadget
Money, paper
Motion
Mouth
Movement or travel, routine
Narrator
Near relative
Needle
Neighborhood interest
Neighborhood activity
Neighborhood
Nerves
Nervous system and illness
Nervous disease
Nervous aggravation
Nervousness
News, those who bring
News, receiving
News
Newspaper
Notary
Nutrition
Opinion
Orator
Paper
Parrot
Parsley herb
Patent
People who give service
Peptic ulcer
Perceive
Perception
Periodical
Perjury
Person employed in a trade
Persuasive
Pest

Pet
Petty
Phone call
Photograph
Pin
Pneumonia
Poet
Porcelain
Post office
Postal system
Precision
Press
Preventative medicine
Printer
Printing
Printing press
Promissory note
Public works
Pupil
Question
Quicksilver
Rabbi
Radio as communication
Railroad
Rationalization
Reason
Reasoning ability
Record keeper
Reflex
Relative
Report
Reporter
Respiratory system
Road
Roller skate
Rumors and lies
Sales
Salesperson
Scholar
School, elementary
School
Schooling
Schoolmate
Secretary
Seeing
Servant
Service rendered or received
Service, volunteer
Service, military
Service repair person
Sewing machine
Sibling
Sight, sense of
Sign that is read
Sign papers
Sister
Skin condition
Sled
Solar plexus
Speaker
Speaking
Speech
Squirrel
Stammering
Statement
Stationer
Stenographer
Stenography
Street
Student
Studies
Study, love of
Study
Subordinate role
Surgical supplies
Surveying equipment
Take for granted
Talk
Talkative, overly
Talker
Talking
Tape recorder
Teacher
Teaching
Teenager
Telegram
Telegraph
Telephone system
Telephone
Tenants and lodgers
Tennis
Test, written or oral
Theory
Therapeutic activity
Thermostat
Thief
Thin, clear optics
Thoughts
Ticket
Tongue disease
Tongue
Tourist
Trade
Traffic
Train
Transit
Transmission
Transport worker
Transport
Transportation, means of
Transportation
Travel, local
Travel agent
Trifle
Trip
Trip, short
Trivial matter
Trumpet
Tuberculosis
Turquoise stone
Typewriter
Typist
Understanding
Usurer
Vacillation
Vehicle
Vehicle, small and light
Ventilation
Verbosity
Versatility
Vertigo
Veterinarian
Virgin
Visit
Visitor
Vitamin
Waitress
Walnut tree
Wednesday
Wheat
Wit
Witness
Words
Work
Work habits
Work requiring wit or intelligence
Work area

Worker in any trade
Workers
Working environment
Working class
Writer
Writing
Writing skill
Writing talent
Writing tools
Written document
Young people
Youth

# Venus

Ability to handle funds
Acting
Actor
Adolescent
Adornment
Adultery
Advancement, economical
Aesthetics
Affairs of the heart
Affection
Affectionate matters
Agreement
Alabaster stone
Alliance
Almond tree
Amusements
Apple tree
Appreciation
Apricot tree
Architect
Art
Art dealer
Artist
Artistic talent
Artistic pursuit
Arts, fine
Asset, liquid or monetary
Asset, tangible
Back, lower
Balance
Bank
Banker
Beautician
Beautification
Beauty, things of
Beauty
Bed
Bedroom
Beloved pet
Beryl stone
Bladder disorder
Blood, circulation of
Blood clot
Blood, venous

Bond with others
Botanist
Brass metal
Bronze
Budget
Calf
Calm things down
Candy
Cash register
Cash flow
Cash at hand
Cat
Cattle rancher
Cattle market
Chakra, fifth, blue
Charm
Checkbook
Checking account
Cheerfulness
Choir
Chrysolite stone
Circulation, stoppage of blood
Claw
Clothing, evening
Clove herb
Club, social
Coin
Color
Color, deep blue
Color, pale blue
Color, azure blue
Color, violet
Comfort
Commodity
Companionship
Competition
Compromise
Concert
Confectionery
Congenial area
Constipation
Consummation
Contest
Contract between partners

Contract, legal or social
Contractual agreement
Cooperation with others
Cooperative arrangement
Copper, metal
Coral stone
Cosmetician
Cosmetics
Counselors
Court of law
Courtship
Creative talents
Culture
Custom
Cypress tree
Dancer
Dancing
Date
Death of another
Decorative arts
Decorator
Deer
Designer
Desirability
Diabetes
Dining room
Diphtheria
Diplomacy
Diplomat
Dolphin
Dove
Drama
Dressmaker
Ear
Earnings capacity
Earnings
Economy
Effeminate
Elderberry herb
Embroidery
Emerald stone
Emotional attachment
Enemy, open
Engraver

*Astrological Keywords*

Enjoyment
Entertainer
Entertainment
Fairness
Favors
Female relations
Female occupation
Finances
Financial matters
Fine arts
Finery
Flings and love affairs
Flirtation
Florist
Flower
Fortune, good
Friday
Fruitful
Fun
Furniture, luxury
Furniture, garden
Furniture
Garden
Gem
Gifts and legacies
Glove
Goldenrod herb
Goods on a shelf
Grace
Guestroom
Handicrafts
Harmony through mental activity
Harmony
Herb, delicate
Honey
Honeymoon
Illness
Inner resources of the self
Investment
Investments, sound
Jewelers
Jewelry
Jewelry as wealth
Joint venture
Judge presiding
Kidney
Laces
Lazy
Leisure

Linens, fine household
Loss or gain
Loss, financial
Lost items in general
Lost thing
Love
Love affair
Love of pleasure
Luck
Luxury
Lying
Lymphatic system
Marriage and unions of all kinds
Meditation
Mental levels Income
Merriment
Merriment
Middle level
Missing thing
Missing things Increase
Mistress Indolence
Mistress
Money
Money belonging to querent
Moral character
Mothers
Mothers
Movable physicians
Movable possessions
Museums
Museums
Music
Musical instrument, stringed
Musical instrument
Musician, entertainer
Nephew
Nick
Niece
Normal
Nurse
Nutrition
Object of affection
Orchestra
Ornament
Ovary
Painter (artist)
Partner
Partnership
Party

Pastel
Peach
Pennyroyal
People, society
Peppermint herb
Performer
Perfumer
Personal belongings
Personal wealth
Personal jewelry
Pharynx
Pink
Plant
Plate
Play for fun
Player
Pleasurable pursuit
Pleasure
Pocketbook
Poetry
Possession, movable
Profit or gain
Property, movable
Public relations
Public street
Purse
Rabbit
Recreation
Relationship, committed
Relationship, contractual
Relationship, happy
Relationship, interpersonal
Resources, personal
Restaurant
Right
Ring
Romance
Royalty
Safe
Safe-deposit boxes
Sapphire stone
Satisfaction
Satisfying others
Savings
Securities
Securities, negotiable
Sensuality, not sex
Sentimentality
Sex

Sex, recreational
Silk
Singer
Singing
Skin condition
Sloppy
Social affair
Social contact
Social graces
Social life
Social urges
Softly curved object
Sorrel herb
Spearman herb
Spouse
Stock exchange
Stolen thing
Stylish clothing
Substance
Sugar
Sweetheart
Sweets
Talent
Tangible asset
Taste, good
Teamwork
Tenderness
Theatrics
Those who cater to pleasure
Throat
Thyme herb
Tonsillitis
Tonsils
Treaty
Tree
Trousseau
Union of two people
Urge to adapt to others
Vacation
Valuables
Values
Vanity
Vein
Virgin
Vocal cord
Wallet
Wardrobe
Wealth
Whatever gratifies the senses

Wife
Wine, sweet
Women
Women, young
Women's articles
Women's clothing
Woodpile
Woods, enameled
Yoke
Young girl
Young people

# Mars

A.I.D.S.
Abortion, surgical
Abrasion
Accident
Accident, liability of
Action
Activity
Acute fever
Adventurer
Aggression
Aggressor
Anger
Argument
Armed services
Arms fire
Army
Arrogance
Assertion
Assertiveness
Athletic contest
Athletics
Automobile
Bailiff
Barber
Basil herb
Battle
Beginning, new
Blacksmith
Bladder disorder
Bladder
Blister
Blood disease
Bloodshed
Bloodstone stone
Blow inflicted by force
Boot
Borage herb
Brain
Breakage
Brutality
Burglar
Burn
Burning
Butcher

Cactus
Carpenter
Cayenne herb
Cemetery worker
Chakra, first, red
Chemist
Chimney
Coffee
Color, drab brown
Color, purple
Color, red
Color, scarlett
Combat
Competition
Conquest
Construction
Coroner
Cosmetic surgery
Courage
Crematory
Cruelty
Cut
Cutting
Danger
Daring
Death
Defiance
Dentist and dentistry
Desire
Desk
Distemper
Doer
Drum
Duel
Eagle
Ear, left
Effort to get ahead
Energy
Engineer
Engineering
Enthusiasm
Epidemic
Explosive
External sex organ

Face injury
Face
Fever
Fighter
Fire fighter
Fire
Firearm
Fireplace
Force
Forge
Furnace
Garlic
Garnet stone
Ginseng herb
Guard
Gun shooter
Gun
Hate
Hawk
Head of body
Hemorrhage
Herb, pungent
Hops herb
House, driest part of
Hunter
Imprudent
Incest
Inflammation
Inflammatory disease
Initiative
Injury
Inoculation
Insect, stinging
Instrument, percussion
Instrument
Instrument, sharp
Iron
Iron, things made of
Ironworker
Junk
Khaki cloth
Knives and sharp instruments
Lamb
Leadership

Astrological Keywords

Leukemia, acute
Liability to accident
Libido
Liquor
Machine
Machinery
Machinist
Mahogany
Male sex drive
Manufacturing
Marriage
Mathematical ability
Mechanic
Mechanical ability
Mechanical occupation
Mechanical thing
Men ages 25 to 35
Men, young
Metal worker
Military
Money of others
Mortality
Motion
Mover
Muscle
Muscular system
Mustard seed
Needle
Nettle herb
Onion
Operation
Oven
Paramedic
Parsley herb
Passion
Penetration
Peppermint herb
Peril
Person of mature age
Pestilence
Pioneer
Plague
Police
Potency
Power
Probe
Quarrelsome
Radish
Rape
Rashness
Recklessness
Reddish complexion
Redwood
Rhubarb
Rival
Robber
Scald
Self-assertion
Self-confidence
Selfhood
Sensual
Sex
Sex organ
Sexual disease
Sexual energy
Sexual nature
Sexual power
Sexuality
Sheep
Sheep farmer
Shepherd
Sheriff
Slaughterhouse
Sleep
Smith
Soldier
Spark of life
Spontaneity
Sports
Sports arena
Stab
Steel
Steel worker
Stir things up
Strength
Strife
Surgeon
Surgery
Sword
Task involving danger or adventure
Taste
Temper, quick
Thing with sharp angles
Those in armed forces
Thrust
Tiger ruby stone
Tool
Tuesday
Turbulence
Venereal disease
Venture
Venture, new
Vigor
Violence
Violent crime
Virility
War
Weapon
Work
Work with fire
Work with iron or steel
Work with sharp instrument
Wound
Young men

# Jupiter

Abstraction
Academia
Advanced degree
Advancement, economic
Advertisement
Affluence
Almond
Alter
Altruism
Amethyst stone
Animal, large or wild
Animal, fondness for
Anything that expands horizons
Anything that protrudes
Archery
Artery
Asparagus
Astrology, horary
Attic
Award
Bail, get out on
Balcony
Banker
Bay herb
Belief system
Berries
Bible
Bilberry herb
Birch tree
Blessing
Blood
Blood, circulation of the
Blood disease
Blood pressure, high
Boil
Bond
Bouncy
Broker
Brother, younger
Bus
Businessperson, big
Buttocks
Capitalism
Carbuncle stone

Ceremony that legalizes a matter
Chakra, second, orange
Charitable institution
Charity given and received
Chicory herb
Church
Churchperson
Circulatory system
Clergy
Clergyperson
Clove herb
Code of ethics
College
Color, ashen
Color, wine
Color, magenta
Color, yellow green
Color, blue violet
Color, purple
Color, violet
Color, spotted
Color, blue
Compass
Conceptual framework
Convocation
Counselor
Court of law
Court of justice
Cultural knowledge
Current
Dandelion herb
Diabetes
Diplomat
Disease caused by excess
Divination
Doctor of civil law
Education
Education, higher
Education, adult class
Educator
Elephant
Embezzle
Entrepreneur
Escape from penalty

Escape from bondage
Ethics
Excess
Expansion
Expansiveness
Fairness
Faith
Favor
Finances
Financial abundance
Forecasting
Foreign affairs
Foreigner
Fortune, good
Fortune
Freedom
Freedom, concept of
Friendship
Fruit
Fur
Furniture
Future, predicting of
Gambling
Gambling, lottery and wheels
Game preserve
Generosity
Golfer
Graduation cap and gown
Growth
Guru
Handle another's possession
Height
Herb, sweet
Hip
Holy object
Honesty
Honey
Honor and code of ethics
Horse breeder
Horse
Horse racing
Humor
Hunting
Hyssop herb

Astrological Keywords

Increase
Indulgence
Instrument, delicate
Insurance
Intellectual pursuit
Jaundice
Jockey
Journey
Journey of partner
Journey to distant place
Judge
Judge's gavel
Jurisprudence
Justice
Large institution
Large, full object
Large financial institution
Lavish expenditure
Law, the
Lawyers as a class
Lecture
Legal profession
Legal action
Legalize by ceremony or ritual
Leisure
Liberality
Liberty
Library, great
Literature
Liver
Liver disease
Luck
Lucky break
Machinery that brings gain
Mania
Mansions and estates, great
Master bedroom
Medical profession
Men's clothing
Metal
Middle-aged person
Mind, higher
Minister, clergy
Morality
Mountain
Mountain climber
Nutrition
Obesity
Opportunity

Optimism
Parade float
Parole
People aged 45-60
People of higher status
Philanthropic institution
Philanthropic reasoning
Philosopher
Philosophy
Physician
Politician
Politics
Porch
Preacher
Prestige
Priest
Prize
Professional
Professional work
Profit or gain
Propaganda
Prophecy
Prophet
Prosperity
Protection
Psychologist
Public convention
Publicity director
Publicity
Publisher
Publishing
Race horse
Race track
Religious
Reprieve
Republican
Rewards
Riches
Robe
Rosary
Rubber
Sage herb
Salesmanship
Sapphire stone
Scholar
Sciatic nerve
Senator
Shipping business
Sound judgment

Speculation
Sports
Sportsperson
Stranger
Student at a university
Success
Synod
Systematic thinking
Theologian
Thigh
Those in a confidential position
Those of wealth and influence
Thursday
Tin metal
Trade
Train
Travel, long distance
Traveler, world
Tree, orchard
Tree, shade
Trial lawyer
Trip, long or distant
Truth
Tumor
Uncle, maternal
Uncle, paternal
Undeserved reward
Uniform
University
Upper level
Valuables
Vehicle, large
Vein
Velvet
Voyage
Waiter
Wart
Wealth
Welfare worker
Whale
Wholesaler
Wig
Willingness to gather experience
Wine, heavy
Winnings
Wisdom
World view
Worldwide contact

# Saturn

Achievement
Administrator
Afraid
Agate stone
Aging
Agriculture
Air conditioning
Ambition
Ancestor
Ancient matters
Archaeology
Armor
Artery, hardening of
Arthritis
Atrophy
Attainment
Authority and authority figure
Bankrupt
Barley
Basement
Basic utility
Beam, wooden
Bear
Beggar
Bigot
Binding
Binds, anything that
Bird of prey
Blackness
Blow inflicted by force
Blunt instrument
Bondage
Bone
Boss
Boundary
Brick
Brick layer
Bringing to justice
Brooding
Builder
Business person
Calamity
Calendar
Calf
Camphor herb
Carbon
Career, capacity for
Caution
Cellar
Cement
Cemetery
Ceramics
Chain
Chairman of the board
Chief executive
Chimney sweeper
Chiropractor
Choking
Chronic illness
Circulation, stoppage of blood
Civil servant
Civil lawyer
Civil service
Clock
Clown
Clown costume
Club, as an instrument
Coagulate
Coal
Coffin
Cold
Coldest part of the house
Coldness
Color, black
Color, dark brown
Color, indigo
Comfrey herb
Compressed
Concentration
Concrete structure
Conservation
Conservatism
Constipation
Contraction
Contractor
Conventionality
Cork
Corporation
Cough
Crystal stone
Cultivator
Cyprus tree
Danger
Dark place
Deafness
Death
Debt
Decay
Defeat
Delay
Democrat
Denim
Dental problem
Depression
Deprivation
Depth
Destroyer
Diamond stone
Disadvantage
Discipline, those who enforce it
Discipline
Disheartening
Dishonor
Dissipation of energy
Doom
Door
Dullness
Dump
Duty
Ear, right
Earth
Ebony
Economist
Elder
Elderly
Embargo
Employer
Employment
Endurance
Envy
Ephemeris
Equipment, stable

*Astrological Keywords*

Executive
Executive acumen
Facing reality
Failure
Fall
Fall from power
Famine
Farmer
Father
Fatigue
Fears and worries
Fence
Financial obligations of the querent
Flint stone
Foreperson
Form
Fossil
Foundation
Foundation of building
Frustration that causes illness
Frustration
Funeral
Gardener
Genealogy
Glue
Goat
Governing authority
Government
Granite stone
Gravity
Grim reaper
Guardian
Hammer
Hard work
Hardship
Health, poor
Hearing, sense of
Hearse
Heartening
Heavy thing
Herder
Hide of animal
Hindering factor
History
Ice
Illness, chronic
India and its people
Inhibition
Insanity, danger of

Integrity
Introspective
Ivory
Jackass
Jealousy
Jesuit
Junk
Justice
Karma
Knee
Labor
Laborious matter
Lack
Lack of circulation
Land
Landlord
Landowner
Large wood structure
Large tree
Law of society
Lead
Leather goods
Leather
Letter merchant
Leukemia, chronic
Liability, financial
Limitation
Limiting condition
Limits
Linoleum
Loss in general
Lower-level
Manager
Manure pile
Mason
Masonry
Mathematician
Mayor
Melancholy
Member of a wedding
Men from the past
Merriment
Methodical
Mine
Miser
Misfortune
Monk
Monument
Mortality

Mortgage
Necessity
Obligation
Obstacle
Obstruction
Occupation, poorly paid
Office
Official
Official business
Old age
Order
Organization
Organizational ability
Organizational ability
Orthodoxy
Outer limit
Overalls
Paralysis
Patience
People aged 60-70
Peril
Perseverance
Person, older
Person of mature age
Person, serious
Person, conservative
Person, old
Pessimism
Pewter
Plumber
Plumbing supplies
Position in society
Pottery
Poverty
Practical
Pragmatic
Priest
Prison
Prudence
Puritanism
Quarry
Quartz stone
Quiet
Ranch
Real estate
Realtor
Receptivity
Refrigerate
Relationship, protracted

Remorse
Reserve
Responsibility
Restraint
Restricting condition
Retirement
Retreat
Rheumatism
Rock
Rodent
Rope
Routine
Rubber
Ruins
Ruler
Salt
Sapphire stone
Saturday
Scientific law
Sedative
Selfishness
Sense of lack
Serious
Seriousness
Shoe
Shovel
Shrewdness
Skeleton
Skin
Skin condition
Slow down
Slowness
Smother, things that
Snake
Solidification
Solitude
Sorrows
Spider
Spinach
Spinal trouble
Spleen
Stability
Stabilizing influence
Stairs
Starvation
Static condition
Stockholder
Stone
Strangulation

Stricture
Structure
Suffocation
Superior
Suspicious
Teacher
Teeth
Tester, the
Tests and tribulations
Theory
Those in a responsible position
Tile
Time
Time, productive use of
Timing
Toothache
Toxic waste, deposit of
Tradition
Tragedy
Tramp
Truck
Truth
Undertaker
Unused area
Upsetting condition
Urge for security
Vehicle, garbage and rubbish
Wall
Warden in a prison
Weighing machine
Weight
Wheelbarrow
Wine, dry
Wisdom gained from experience
Wisdom
Wood, thing made of
Wood, petrified
Wool
Work
Work, commonly avoided
Worldly position
Worries
Yesterday
Yoke

# Uranus

Abortion, spontaneous
Accident
Acquaintance
Advanced thinking
Advisors as a class
Affiliation in group
Agitation
Aircraft
Airplane
Amber stone
Ankle
Anything electronic
Associate
Astrologer
Astrological affairs
Astrology
Astrology, horary
Astronomy
Aura
Automobile
Autonomy
Aviation
Awakener, the
Battery
Bicycle
Blood, circulation of
Bloodstone stone
Bohemian
Bomb
Break free
Break
Broadcast
Business deal, big
Calf of the body
Car
Carnelian stone
Castration
Cesarean
Change, sudden
Circulatory system
Clairvoyance
Clock
Color, checked
Color, electric blue
Color, mixed or streaked
Color, multicolor or plaid things
Commission
Commoner
Communication, one way
Computer
Computer technician
Computer operation
Congress
Counselor
Cramps
Cranks and crackpots
Cyclone
Death, sudden
Defiance
Detachment
Detour
Deviation from the norm
Dictator
Disruption
Divorce
Dynamite
Earthquake
Eccentric
Egotistical
Electric
Electrical appliance
Electrical engineer
Electrician
Electricity
Electricity
Emancipation
Enemy, secret
Escape from bondage
Estrangement
Excitement
Exciting place
Explosion
Flying
Freedom loving
Freedom, concept of
Freedom
Friendship
Friendship, ties of
Fuse box
Futuristic
Garage
Gas
Generator
Genius
Ghost
Group activity
Hallucinations
Ham radio
Hanger
Hearing device
Heavy artillery
Helicopter
Hippie
Homosexuality
Humanitarian
Humanitarian activities and ideals
Idea, new
Illegal
Illegitimacy
Illness, incurable
Independence
Individualism
Industrial Revolution
Infamy
Ingenious
Ingenuity
Innovation
Intellect, intuitive
Invention
Inventiveness
Key
Kinetic
Labor union
Labor strike
Laboratory
Lawbreaker
Lecturer
Liberty
Light
Lightning
Magic
Magician

Astrological Keywords

Magnetic
Marriage, separation in
Mass media
Meddlesome
Mental strain
Metamorphosis
Microscope
Miscarriage
Misfortune, unexpected
Mob
Modern gadget
Movie
Natural disaster
Nervous aggravation
Nervous twitch
Nervous breakdown
Nervous tension
Nervous system and illness
Nervousness
New method
New Age
New age gadget
News, circulation of
Nomadic Intellectual
Non-conformist
Notorious
Novelty
Occult
Odd shaped thing
Originality
Outer space
Outlaw
Paralysis
Parliament
People, eccentric
People, unusual
People age 70-85
Perversity
Pilot
Plaid
Professional association
Psychiatrist
Psychological counselor
Psychologist
Psychology
Radical idea
Radical
Radio
Radio broadcasting

Radioactivity
Radium
Rebel
Rebellion
Relationship, break in
Reorganization
Repellent
Revolution
Rocket
Rupture
Russia
Science fiction
Scientist
Sedative
Separation
Sexual perversion
Shock
Social alliance
Society
Spaceship
Spark
Spasmodic
Spontaneity
Storm
Storm, violent
Strike, labor
Sudden or unexpected events
Sudden break
Sudden act of God
Surprise
Technical ability
Technician
Telegraph
Telepathy
Telephone
Telephone call
Telephone system
Telescope
Television
Thinker, free
Thinking, progressive
Tornado
Tractor
Tradition breaker
Tragedy
Travel by air
Turbulence
Uncommon pursuit
Unexpected obstacle

Unexpected
Unforeseeable
Unique thing
Unstable area
Unusual happening
Unusual method
Upset
Uranium
Utopia
Vapor
Vehicle
Vehicle speed
Ventilation
Wind damage
Wind, circulation of
Wire, high powered
Women's liberation
X-ray

# Neptune

Abnormal person
Acting
Actor
Addict
Alcohol
Alcohol, those whose work is connected with
Alcoholism
Amethyst stone
Anemia
Anesthesia
Aquamarine stone
Artificial limb
Artist
Ascetics
Assassination
Astrology, horary
Bacteria
Ballet
Ballet dancer
Bankruptcy
Bath
Beach
Beautification
Beryl stone
Betrayal
Beverage
Bigamist
Bisexuality
Blackmail
Bribery
Camera
Camouflage
Catalepsy
Chakra, sixth, indigo
Chakra
Chaos
Character defect
Charitable institution
Charity
Charity given and received
Charity
Cheat
Chemical warfare
Chemical
Chemist
Chemistry
Children, out-of-wedlock
Choking
Christianity
Clairvoyance
Clam
Clandestine
Clandestine work
Clandestine affairs
Cloudiness
Color, white
Color, mauve
Color, sea green
Color, lavender
Color, iridescent
Coma
Communism
Compassion
Con artist
Concentration camp
Concern for another
Confidence
Confidential matter
Confusion
Conspiracy
Contrition
Coral stone
Counterfeit
Crime
Criminal, those who work with
Crying
Crystal ball
Dancing
Daydreaming
Deception
Defeat
Defect of character
Delay
Delusion
Detention
Devotion
Diffusion
Displaced person
Dissolution of boundary
Dissolving
Dreamer
Dreams and visions
Drink trade
Drowning
Drug
Drug addiction
Drug dealer
Drug
Drug, illicit
Drunkard
E.S.P.
Embezzlement
Emotional problem
Endocrine gland
Environmental pollution
Equipment, scientific
Error in judgment
Escapism
Esthetic sensibility
Estrangement
Evasion
Exaggeration
Fabric, transparent (nets and veils)
Failure
Faith
False appearance
False teeth
Fan
Fantasy
Feet
Fiddle
Film actor
Film
Fine arts
Fish
Fisher
Flattery
Fog
Force inclining to dissolution
Forgetfulness
Fragrance

Fraud
Fraudulent scheme, grand
Frustration that causes illness
Frustration
Gas
Gasoline
Gelatin
Ghetto
Glamour
Glass
Grief
Gullible
Hallucination
Hearing aid
Hindering factor
Hospital
Hot tub
Hunch
Hydrogen
Hydrotherapy
Hypersensitivity
Hypnosis
Hypnotist
Hypochondriac
Hypodermic
Hysteria
Idealism
Ideals
Illness, incurable
Illusion
Image
Imagination
Imaginative ability
Impotence
Impractical idea
Incense
Infectious substance
Inspiration
Intangible
Intrigue
Intuition
Israel, state of
Journey by water
Junk
Kelp
Kerosene
Large boat
Lavender
Leak, water

Lies and rumors
Limiting condition
Liquid
Maladjustment, psychological
Manure pile
Marine
Martyrdom
Medicine
Mediumistic
Mental health worker
Mental illness
Mermaid
Mindedness, absent
Mirage
Miscarriage, danger from
Misfortune
Misfortune, unexpected
Misinformation
Misrepresentation
Mist
Moron
Morphine
Motion picture
Movie
Music
Musician, entertainer
Mysterious condition
Mysterious location
Mystery
Mystic
Mysticism
Myth
Naïve
Narcotic
Navigation
Navigator
Navy
Nervous breakdown
Nudist
Obscure
Obsession
Occupation involving unreality
Ocean
Oil
Oil well
Opiate
Oracle
Orphan
Orphanage

Paint
Painter
Painter, artistic
Paranoia
Past mistake
Pearl stone
People, sensitive
Personal limitation
Perversity
Petroleum
Philanthropic institution
Philosopher
Photographer
Photography
Photography supplies
Pilot
Pipe dream
Plastic
Plumbing problem, leak
Poetry, love of
Poetry and poet
Poison
Political propaganda
POW camp
Pretense
Prison
Prison system
Problem, personal
Propaganda
Prophecy
Psychic phenomenon
Psychic
Psychic ability
Quietude
Rain
Receptivity
Recluse
Relationship, hidden
Renunciation
Replacement for something else
Research
Retreat
Sacrifice
Sailor
Saint
Salt
Scheme and schemer
Sea
Seafaring

Séance
Seclusion
Secret fear
Secret
Secret sorrow
Seduce
Seeing, not clearly
Self-analysis
Self-deception
Self-destruction
Self-pity
Self-restraint
Self-sacrifice
Self-undoing
Selfless giving
Septic tank
Service, selfless
Serving mankind
Sexual perversion
Ship
Shipping
Sin of omission and commission
Skeleton in the closet
Slave
Sleep
Sleepwalking
Smoke
Solitude
Somnambulism
Sorcerer
Sorrow
Sorry for
Spiritual progress
Spiritual matter
Spirituality
Spy
Stage
Stained glass
Strategy
Submarine
Submerging
Substitute
Subversion
Suffocation
Suicide
Surrender
Swim
Swimming pool
Swindler
Sympathy
Tea
Television
Thing that engulfs
Those in the film industry
Those who work with liquids
Time to be alone
Tobacco
Trance
Treason
Tree, bonsai or dwarf
Turmoil, inner or psychic
Ulterior motive
Undisclosed condition
Undoing
Unrealistic
Unreality
Vagueness
Vandalism
Vehicle, modern
Visionary
Wanderlust
Washing machine
Wasting disease
Water damage
Water tank
Welfare
Welfare program
Where you reflect or meditate
Widowhood
Window, major
Work with oil
Work behind the scenes
Work done quietly or alone
Work with liquids
Writer
Yacht
Yogi

# Pluto

A.I.D.S.
Abortion, surgical
Abuse
Abyss
Accomplice
Alchemy
Alone
Ambush
Amnesia
Analysis
Analytical scientist
Anarchist
Anarchy
Anonymity
Ant
Armadillo
Atomic bomb
Atomic power
Atomic energy
Atomic scientist
Bacteria
Bedroom
Beginnings and endings
Beginnings, new
Betrayal
Birth
Bladder disorder
Bladder
Blow inflicted by force
Bomb
Bondage
Bowel, lower
Brutality
Butcher
C.I.A.
Chakra, seventh, violet
Chemical
Cleaning out
Clearing away
Cockroach
Coercion
Color, blue
Compelling force
Complication
Compulsion
Compulsive sex
Compulsory cooperation
Conception
Constipation
Convent
Coroner
Corpse
Covert
Crematories
Crime
Criminal action
Crocodile
Cruelty
Dancers
Danger
Death and regeneration
Death, physical and spiritual
Decay
Decaying matters
Degeneration
Destruction
Detective
Dictator
Dictatorship
Digging up
Disappearance
Domination
Drastic event
Dreams and visions
Drug
Drug addiction
Dump
Ejection
Elimination
Ending
Enemy, secret
Epidemic
Espionage
Excrement
External sex organs
Extremes
F.B.I.
Fate
Fisher
Flea
Fog
Force
Fraud
Funeral
Gallbladder
Gangster
Garbage can
Garbage disposal
Genital disorder
Ghost
Gout
Government
Group as a source of power
Growth, slow
Gun shooter
Hallucination
Healer
Healing
Healing power
Hidden thing
Hospital
Hot tub
Ice
Iguana
Incest
Inoculation, mass
Inquisition
Inquisitor
Inside of thing
Intensity
Investigator
Isolation
Junk
Junk dealer
Junkyard
Kidnapper
Kidnapping
Liver
Lizard
Lust
Magic
Main bathroom

Astrological Keywords

Main sewer outlet
Manager
Manipulation of another
Martyrdom
Mass of people
Mass action
Mass production
Metamorphosis
Mind, subconscious
Mine, hidden wealth in
Money of another
Monk
Mortality
Mortgage
Mosquito
Movie
Murder
Nun
Obsession
Occult matters
Oil
Organized crime
Penetration
Peril
Person, forcible control of
Pet, peculiar
Phobia
Physician
Plague
Plot
Plumber
Plumbing
Police, secret
Political underground
Pollution
Power
Printing
Probe
Prostate gland
Psychoanalysis
Psychological counselor
Psychologist
Psychology, depth
Purge
Purification
Race of people
Rape
Rapist
Rat
Rebirth
Rectum
Recuperation, power of
Refuse
Regeneration
Reincarnation
Rejuvenation
Renewal
Renewed or restored thing
Renovation
Reptile, armored
Research
Researcher
Routine, odd and complicated
Rubbish
Salvage
Secret agreement to defraud
    the public
Secret police
Secrets
Seed
Septic tank
Sewer
Sex
Sex organ
Sexual disease
Sexual merging
Sexual power
Sexual release
Sexuality
Shrewdness
Snake
Social change
Spermatozoa and ova
Spiritual rebirth
Spy
Steam
Steam bath
Suicide
Surgeon
Surgery
Suspicion
Tax evasion
Termite
Terrorist
Those who work beneath the
    surface
Toxic waste
Transformation
Transmutation
Treasure, buried
Tumor
Turtle
Tyrant
Undertaker
Underworld
Underworld character
Unearthing
Uniformed worker
Unwilling conformity
Upheaval
Vacancy
Venereal disease
Vermin
Violent crime
Violent
Virus
Vulture
War
Wasp
Waste and those who waste
Waste

# Aspects

Conjunction
    Concentration
    Union of Planets
    Venture, new
Conjunction and Parallel
    Activity, new
    Intensification
    Binding
Inconjunct
    Adjustment
    Lack of perspective
    Discord
    Need for change
Opposition
    Destructive
    Awareness
    Obstacles
Quincunx
    Challenging
    Redirecting
    Diverting
Semi-sextile
    Growth
    Unseen opportunity
    Reactive
    Lack of ease
Sesquiquadrate
    Abrasive
    Agitation
    Stressful
    Harsh
Semi-square
    Irritating
    Minor stress
    Tension
    Friction
Sextile
    Affability
    Attraction
    Sextile
Square
    Accomplishment
    Tension
    Challenging
    Conflicting
Trine
    Ease
    Comfort
    Harmony
    Idealism

# Part of Fortune

Cash on hand
Earnings
Finances
Financial matters
Fortune, good
Income
Loss or gain
Loss financial (in eighth house)
Lost items in general
Lost things
Resourceful personnel
Stolen things (in eighth house)

# Asteroids and Nodes

**Chiron**
Wisdom
Patience
Suffering, relieve of others
Healer of others
Unique expression
Healer may not be able to heal self
Behavior, unique

**Ceres**
Grain
Harvest
Animal, caring for
Physical constitution
Parent-child relationship
Herb
Fertility
Mothering, physical
Food
Agriculture
Nurturing
Relationship, family
Nutrition
Comfort, where one provides
Rights, defense of personal

**Juno**
Partner, focus on
Marriage, the partner one needs
Jealousy
Fear of abandonment
Relationship
Love, true
Fairness
Diplomacy
Competing

**Lilith**
Rejection
Divided loyalty
Favoritism
Gender stereotype
Sex, use of dominance
Sexual caring for partner

**Pallas**
Sex, deeply transformative
Perceptual skill
Political strategy
Honor
Respect
Relating, deeper level

**Vesta**
Independent
Sex, more mental or spiritual than physical
Commitment to work
Hard work
Impersonal

**North Node**
Positive objective
Soul's destiny
Spiritual growth
Confidence
Receives, where one
Added confidence

**South Node**
Easy way out with no growth
Past
Karma
Challenges one keeps trying to overcome
Taking the easy way out
Give, where one must
Letting go
Release

# References

Hall, Manly P., *Astrological Keywords*

Goldstein-Jacobson, Ivy M., *Simplified Horary Astrology*

Grell, Paul R., *Keywords*

Wilson, James, *A Complete Dictionary of Astrology*

George, Llewellyn, *The New A to Z Horoscope Maker and Delineator*

J.D., *Astrological Keyword System of Analyzing Character and Destiny*

Woolfolk, Joanna Martine, *The Only Astrology Book You'll Ever Need*

March, Marion D. and McEvers, Joan, *The Only Way to Learn Astrology series*

Hall, Judy, *The Astrology Bible: The Definitive Guide to the Zodiac*

Goodman, Linda, *Love Signs: A New Approach to the Human Heart*

Coley, Henry, *Key to Astrology*

Culpeper, Nicholas, *Astrological Judgment of Disease*

Darrow, Joseph, *The Keyword System*

Heindel, Max, and Foss, Augusta, *The Message of the Stars*

Heindel, Max, and Foss, Augusta, *Simplified Scientific Astrology*

Erlewine, Michael, *Keywords*

Lang-Wescott, Martha, *Asteroids*